FRAME THIS

ORACLE

*A Tool to
Deepen Your
Card Readings
and Reframe
Your
Perspective*

JUNO LUCINA
Illustrated by Dan Goodfellow

Other Schiffer Books by the Author:

Iago's Penumbra: A Metaphysical Novel, ISBN 978-0-7643-6632-1
The Alchemy of Tarot, ISBN 978-0-7643-3710-9
The Healing Tarot, ISBN 978-0-7643-4392-6
The Kingdom Within Tarot, ISBN: 978-0-7643-3711-6
Celtic Goddesses, Witches, and Queens Oracle, Danu Forest,
illustrated by Dan Goodfellow, ISBN 978-0-7643-6700-7

Library of Congress Control Number: 2024932158

Type set in Minion/New Frank

ISBN: 978-0-7643-6827-1
Printed in China

Published by REDFeather Mind, Body, Spirit
An imprint of Schiffer Publishing, Ltd.
4880 Lower Valley Road, Atglen, PA 19310
Phone: (610) 593-1777; Fax: (610) 593-2002
Email: Info@redfeathermbs.com
Web: www.redfeathermbs.com

REDFeather™
MIND | BODY | SPIRIT

Printed in China

To Sandalphon,
Thanks for the reframe.

"*Frame This Oracle* provides us with the opportunity to literally and figuratively reframe the meaning of any Tarot or oracle card. Given its current popularity, it is difficult to find this type of innovative approach to cartomancy; however, Lucina has created an exciting, new system with endless possibilities. This is a must-have tool that will enhance your reading skills by encouraging you to embrace fresh ways of seeing and being."

Monica Bodirsky, artist and author of the
Shadowland Tarot, Shadowland Lenormand, Between the
Worlds Oracle, and *The Awakening Tarot*

"*Frame This Oracle* is a rare find. Such a seemingly simple, but truly innovative, idea will readily unleash both your intuition and creativity, encouraging a greater level of self-understanding and perception. These beautifully designed cards can help not only to comprehend the world around you, but, also, to traverse the deeper landscape of your soul."

Steven Bright, author of *Tarot: Your Personal Guide*
and *Inner Eye Oracle*

"A truly amazing and life-enhancing new project from Juno Lucina, with gorgeous art by Dan Goodfellow, *Frame This Oracle* offers a means of enhancing any oracle by placing the user at the centre—literally within a frame that brings the deepest meanings into focus. The freedom of deciding which oracle you use within it opens many doors—or indeed windows, since this is how the author describes them. A wise, brilliant, and thoughtful deck—unlike any other we have seen."

John and Caitlín Matthews, joint and individual
creators of *The Arthurian Tarot, The Wildwood Tarot,*
and *The Time Changer's Tarot*

"*Frame This Oracle* by Juno Lucina and illustrated by Dan Goodfellow is the newest diviner's tool, for using with your favorite cards, charms, or runes or by itself. This unique oracle set is something every collector will want. I haven't seen anything remotely comparable since Emily Carding's *Transparent Tarot*. *Frame This Oracle* is that extra insight into any reading. I will definitely pair them with my own cards. I highly recommend *Frame This Oracle* to everyone."

Julie Cuccia-Watts, author of *Real Sky
Astrology Tarot, Journey into Egypt Tarot,
MAAT Tarot,* and *Ancestral Path Tarot*

"Juno Lucina has created a wonderfully unique tool for the divination world. The deck *Frame This Oracle* will surely elevate the concept of oracles and transcend the conventional. It will guide seekers to expand their readings as well as open up new perspectives. This pack of original frames stands out amidst the vast sea of decks. It offers a doorway to a deeper self-understanding and a dive through mindfulness. *Frame This Oracle* isn't just another addition to the genre; it's an evolution in the divination engine, luring seekers to see beyond the nuances of their existence. Juno lustrously portrays insightful philosophical ideas with each frame, offering clear guidance on how to use it in multiple ways. *Frame This Oracle* is a visual treat that will pull you into a gateway to discovery."

Rana George, author of the bestseller and the
highly acclaimed *The Essential Lenormand: Your Guide to
Precise & Practical Fortunetelling,* and the award-winning
deck *Rana George Lenormand.* She is a teacher,
spiritual counselor, psychic, and medium.

CONTENTS

by PAMELA STEELE

It is exceedingly rare to find a divination modality that is revolutionary, fresh, goal oriented, and profoundly unique. However, miracles do happen, and riding on the crest of this tsunami-sized miracle is *Frame this Oracle*.

This transformative oracle was written by the brilliant author Juno Lucina, whose wisdom and integrity are woven into every word of this book. Her decades of experience in Tarot, teaching, and authoring books have evolved into an extraordinary offering for those who seek truth and authenticity in their lives. The Frames for this masterpiece were illustrated by the remarkably talented UK artist Dan Goodfellow, whose body of work is extensive, insightful, and dynamic. Their combined talents have produced a divination modality that is practical, empowering, and functional.

Frame This Oracle allows you, the Seeker, to remove the artificial barriers we have placed among our bodies, our minds, and our souls. Each card is an actual Frame that you can use to fine-tune your awareness and focus on the details that you might otherwise miss while maintaining your peripheral awareness of what is around you. This is similar to the difference between a scattergun and a laser pointer. *Frame This Oracle* is not going to directly provide you with answers. It is not going to tell you what to do or how to think. Each Frame is carefully crafted to inspire you to look deeply within and is accompanied by relevant questions about what is held within the Frame. This way, rather than giving you a cookie-cutter answer, you are encouraged to dive into your inner knowing and fully experience the information you already possess on a souldeep level. These questions engage your intuition, psychic abilities, and spiritual knowledge to empower you and assist you in achieving self-mastery. Although you may think of yourself as being about as "psychic as a brick," the questions, when answered authentically and honestly, will lead you to follow your true path to enlightenment and wholeness.

Employing and working with this oracle allows you to "Frame the question" and experience firsthand the revelations that come with finding the answers, your answers, within each Frame. Try to think of this adventure in exploration like a scavenger hunt or an Easter egg hunt. Yes, there is great satisfaction in finding the treasures (or the eggs). But what would you discover and learn about yourself if all the prize locations were provided ahead of time? Would you be satisfied and come away feeling fulfilled and content? Would you truly appreciate acquiring these treasures if they were simply given to you? Or would the treasures be sweeter, more appreciated, and thus more valuable if you did the work to find and retrieve them?

This oracle provides you the opportunity to fully experience life happening through you, not to you. The questions asked by Juno in this book are never going to leave you hanging. They are always accompanied by solid advice and suggestions about how to approach what is within the beautifully decorated Frames that you've chosen to work with. *Frame This Oracle* directs your attention inward while utilizing what is around you. Be it divination cards, Tarot cards, oracle cards, photographs, crystals, everyday or sacred objects, or any number of items that stir your imagination or perhaps hint about holding viable information, you will be going beyond duality and entering the realm of quantum reality, where Creation originates. This oracle brings unrealized details into focus by framing them for you to experience material reality and organic creation both as a mortal and an eternal spirit. Juno also provides alternative ways of using your Frames to more fully embrace your evolution and explore the intricacies of you, a Divine Being having a human adventure.

Frame This Oracle was created to empower you, not to make you codependent on outside information or tools. It is designed for daily use to help you clarify what does and does not serve not only who you are now, but who you are becoming. *Frame This Oracle* can be combined with a multitude of other modalities, unique or everyday items, or carried with you to "Frame" your world as you go about your daily life. The only limits are those you put on yourself. *Frame This Oracle* is truly a must-have for those who seek Truth and Wholeness.

Pamela Steele, November 2023
Creator of the *Steele Wizard Tarot: The Language of the Soul, Eternal Seeker Oracle*, and *Wizard's Pets Tarot*

This is a practical oracle.

Sure, it's pretty—pretty to look at, pretty weird, pretty deep, pretty singular. It's nothing like any oracle you've ever seen before.

But it's not just meant to be pretty—this oracle is meant to be read.

Use it. It wants to be used—it calls to you. Can you hear it?

A bit creepy, really.

At first glance, you might think this oracle is full of holes, since every card is a Frame with a big empty space in the middle.

But then, you might be missing the point entirely.

This oracle is full of pointed edges—boundaries that point the way. Each card is a threshold to focus you, direct you to see what you're missing—to understand what's vital. These edges will poke you . . . bother you . . . wake you up in the wee small hours of the morning and wriggle around in your mind, heart, and soul to infiltrate all those dark crevices, cracking wide open those walls to let in . . . not what you think you want, but what you know you need.

It will speak to you. It will help you speak to yourself. It will channel messages from the others who wish to speak.

Only you know if you are ready to listen.

Please listen. We're all waiting for you to see . . .

Everything.

WHY DO WE NEED YET
ANOTHER ORACLE?

After the publication of my two Tarot decks—*The Kingdom Within Tarot* and *The Healing Tarot: 78 Ways to Wellness*—I never intended to make another deck, especially an oracle deck! My Tarot decks and first book on Tarot—*The Alchemy of Tarot: Practical Enlightenment through the Astrology, Qabalah, & Archetypes of Tarot*—contained the sum total of what I wanted to say about Tarot, and I was content to go about writing my novels and living my own singular existence. I never dreamed I might someday feel compelled to create an oracle deck.

Oracle decks have gained remarkably in popularity and seem quite ubiquitous these days. When I began my first tentative exploration of cartomancy with the Tarot, there weren't many Tarot decks to choose from and even fewer oracle decks available—most of which seemed to be by Doreen Virtue (who has since renounced all her new age publications). I looked through a few but found them superficial and lacking in the Tarot's depth and breadth that resonated so deeply with me. I dove into Tarot headfirst and never looked back.

Although I started my divinatory journey with Tarot, I soon added astrology, the I Ching, Lenormand, and crystal gazing to my tools of the trade. I even tried pendulums (though they never really worked for me). When the *Twilight* novels were popular, a friend gifted me *Les Vampires Oracle Cards* by Lucy Cavendish and Jasmine Becket-Griffith, which I viewed as a novelty item at best. I glanced through the doe-eyed ladies on the cards and set them aside in my "what a thoughtful gift" file. A few years later, however, during a particularly tempestuous time in my life, I took them out on a whim (while sipping my second glass of red wine, I might add), and pulled one card at random. The image was artistically appealing, but it was when I read the message about the card that I was cut to the core, for here was the answer I sought and needed in my pain.

The card's message wasn't superficial or lacking in depth at all—it communicated *outside* the scope of Tarot a transmission that definitely needed to be received.

My interest piqued, I expanded my own voyage into the realm of the oracle deck.

My intention was to explore them all, but there are now so many out there that I soon realized this to be a nigh impossible feat. At least half of those I considered didn't speak to me remotely; some even repelled me. Another quarter of the oracle decks seemed solely created to showcase the lovely or stylistic images crafted by a particular artist, yet their guidebooks and my resultant readings contained little substance beyond platitudes, positive affirmations, and ambiguity.

I added a few new oracle decks that inspired me to my collection, and began experimenting with them daily, much as I had initially with the Tarot.

Even the best oracle deck is quite different than a Tarot deck. Most are thematic, generally full of lush, pretty artwork, but each is a one-off creation, entirely dependent upon the solitary abilities of artist and author themselves. With Tarot, once you "know" the seventy-eight card system, the keywords and interpretations, the symbolism and archetypes, the astrological and qabalistic correlations, you can pick up any standard Tarot deck (whether you like the artwork or not) and read them for yourself or another. (If you're not able to do this with a Tarot deck yet, check out my aforementioned book and decks to achieve this proficiency.)

Of course, even with Tarot there is a critical intuitive aspect to every reading, which for some readers is the lion's share of what they utilize to read Tarot; for others, intuition is simply icing on the cake of a firm foundation in system. A third group of readers don't divine at all but use the Tarot and its rich imagery as a sort of Rorschach test to tease the client's own truth out of them.

I still remember the first time I met a truly accurate intuitive reader. She had little of my own background in Tarot, but her precision was uncanny—she is now a dear friend. A gifted psychic, she admitted that she learned Tarot only to give some visual foundation to her psychic premonitions, since she didn't really need the Tarot cards, but sometimes her clients needed to see her doing something tangible during a reading!

By their very nature, oracle readings generally require more intuition from readers than Tarot. Some oracles have quite comprehensive guidebooks and well-conceived systems to help with this, and I have generally found these oracle decks to be the most consistent for reading (*Frame This Oracle* is most definitely this type of oracle).

My own adventures into oracle decks aside, you might ask what prompted me to create yet another cartomancy tool—*especially* an oracle deck?

My favorite oracle decks have changed my life. I have five decks (after sifting through hundreds of them) I use, on a regular basis. Knowing that these five decks are in the world satisfies me, deeply, and I was equally satisfied to use them in my own spiritual practices and remain quiet on the subject.

Until the day came when my oracles and Tarot were unable to confront aspects of existence that wanted to be addressed . . . and then a small, soft nudge woke me in the middle of the night to whisper what might be . . . thereafter a good friend spoke to me about what he hasn't been able to find in his vast divination collection.

And finally, Steven Bright—beloved cartomancy reader and creator—posted this quote on his IG account:

Not every Oracle deck is light and fluffy.
Some have teeth and they're razor-sharp.

Steven Bright

Steven's wise words provided me the audacity I needed to imagine the sharp-toothed oracle I was seeking but hadn't yet found . . .

And so, *Frame This Oracle* was born.

Chomp, chomp.

WHY FRAMES?

Life is much more successfully looked at
from a single window.

F. Scott Fitzgerald

You may not realize it yet, but you are a Frame.

A divine window.

Every person, every body, is a Frame—a focus of being and doing and having in a particular space and time to display for all to see one aspect, one viewpoint, of All That Is—each showcasing one point of beingness that makes up the boundless Being.

Your personal Frame is your own unique individual perspective, your chosen viewpoint as you look out and experience embodiment (and might I add that *very few* of us actually view the world through the Frame of rose-colored glasses). We are singular. We are limited. We can focus on only a few things in any given moment in order to function.

Over time, your Frame becomes more and more solid and sure, on the basis of the stories you are taught, the traumas and triumphs you live through, the people you meet, and the world events that shape your particular place and time upon this earth. Eventually, your Frame inhibits who and what you care about, limits what you focus on, and reflects what you believe, what you recognize (versus actually see or perceive), where you will go, and how you will live.

One of the great marvels of existence is that even as every one of us is a Frame, so we are also creators of Frames, for as we live our lives, we create countless more Frames everywhere we go. (We the created are then blessed with the gift of creation ourselves.)

Our Frames are our viewpoints . . . our foci . . . our perspectives; they determine our aesthetic, purpose, and path. Our Frames organize what we believe, separating them from everything else, helping us focus on what we wish despite the rest.

It's as though your Frames (no matter how consciously or unconsciously chosen) present the version of the world as you wish to see it, as you think others should see it, as you wish others would perceive you and the world, and as you wish you were.

You set apart or *Frame* a part of yourself to present to the world as "you"—it's not that what we choose to display about ourselves isn't true, but what we put in a Frame is definitely an artfully rendered version of ourselves and the world as we wish it to be—or at least what we wish would be perceived. Most of us prefer our own idea of beauty, meaning, and industry, wishing that our own personal aesthetic would be all there is in the world, but of course the truth is quite the contrary.

Social media does a lovely job of helping us Frame ourselves to reach a larger audience, enabling us to hide those things that we do not wish to display—this explains why we love the online world so very much and are drawn to it, almost addictively so.

Most of us are enamored with our Frames; many of us can't even perceive where the Frame ends and the artwork begins anymore.

We *claim* we are being authentic in these aspects of being as we carefully craft our Frames of ourselves and our world, but these window-dressed displays of our impressions, longings, and feelings of the moment are not authentic representations of reality—at best, they are authentic expressions of what we *wish* others would know about us, our ideas, and our internal world. No Frame contains the entirety. If you Frame a picture of a waterfall, it shows us but one interpretation of a waterfall—not the *real* waterfall (if there even is one), not *all* waterfalls, and certainly not the *essence* of what makes a waterfall a waterfall (as opposed to a dog).

Frames never contain the entirety of the topic under consideration or all of what is—and certainly not what all the others believe needs to be Framed—for you can never Frame *everything*—only one thing, a singular viewpoint. The way we Frame things determines not only how they will be received, perceived, and valued, but actually limits what can be perceived by the others at all.

Frames often contain a lie or lies of some sort; these trickster Frames hide something of what is and make us mistake it for what is not. They accomplish this by drawing our attention yet never being the focal point in and of themselves. They are the curtain hiding the man we are supposed to ignore, and many of us use careful framing to misdirect and hide the cracks and holes in our walls. Most of us feel a mighty compulsion to shore up the walls of our beliefs, ideals, and opinions, sure that our lives would be empty and meaningless without them.

When we meet an adult without obvious Frames, they seem incomplete to us somehow, as though something is missing, and they aren't quite fully developed. If all a person's Frames correlate, they seem more finished, refined, and put together. If their Frames don't match, they seem eccentric, messy, and unfinished, as though they still need to sort things out for themselves. Mismatched Frames distract and bother most of us, and chaotic Frames disturb our aesthetic, making us feel unsafe because of the lack of order.

Your Frames (whether physical as they hang on the wall in your home, external as you express your truth and creations outward, or internal in the form of your attention, beliefs, and intentions) convey the message of "you" to the world. What do you love? What are the stories of your life? What you choose to emphasize (Frame) says it all. We might not like to admit the ephemeral nature of our Frames, but many of those we most cherish are subject to the society and time we live in—to some extent, we all are victims of the fashion of the moment, and our Frames reflect our transitory sacred cows.

Just as a physical picture Frame has the initial purpose to protect the artwork it contains, so our Frames protect what we have decided shall and must continue—what we have determined to be true, what we have agreed is sacrosanct, what we have resolved matters. Thus, Frames often separate us from the harsher truths of existence. Our focused viewpoints partition us—we know their familiar (if constricting) edges well, and by contemplating only the subject within the Frame, we are not distracted by what surrounds it. The thicker the Frame, the stronger the barrier (and often narrower the perspective).

Our Frames can provide us powerful concentration and exclusion, with both positive and negative consequences. Every human innovation requires framing to achieve it, yet framing also created all the shadows on the wall of Plato's cave.

Our Frames help us feel as though we are a part of something bigger—our groups and alliances. We align ourselves with those who have similar Frames, and forge connections to have strength and order and safety using our Frames with raised fists and battle cries at the chaos of no distinction (as so many fear death most of all, when all our Frames cease). If our own Framed images match the Framed images of those around us, we believe this makes what we've Framed more possible, more real, more true, more aesthetically beautiful, and more ordered—and so we seek to group and pack together to remake at least the Framed world in our chosen images.

Gather all the Frames of a given group or alliance together, look through them at what they are focused on and showing the world, and you will see a broader vision of the group myth or story as they exist within a larger space or time (or both). Just as we tend to decorate a room to have a similar theme or motif, so when you look at the chosen Frames of a particular group, you'll find they share a similar aesthetic or zeitgeist to their focus and perspective—they all are choosing to live (or trapped, as may be) in a similar room (or prison cell) of their own Framing.

One such Frame, of course, is the *social imaginary*, the collective understanding shared by a community within a particular place and time that underlies their joint stories of how the world should be and how they should live in it based upon their values, institutions, laws, and symbols. This Frames a society's purpose and (it's hoped) a cohesive structure for social life, alas too often irrespective of reality or workability.

Unframed, things are just what they are. Things are born, things live, things die. There is no meaning, no significance, nothing holy, nothing lasts—and so we make our Frames to be able to taste and savor our experiences that pass so quickly into the void from which all arise and to which all return. Our Frames make us feel our lives more intensely—and, by proxy, feel more alive.

Thus, even a memory is a sort of Frame, for we never remember exactly what happened—we remember our experience of what happened, our viewpoint.

Once we remove the Frame from art, once we no longer focus either individually or collectively on a thing, it slowly falls back into the void and ceases to be for us—it is our focused framing that makes things last. Ideas and values so critical in the past are unimportant to us now, and things we consider so vital today and Frame so passionately (viciously) will be discarded as well in the future by our descendants as they Frame new things we either don't value today, take for granted, or haven't yet even imagined.

We all recognize humanity's professional Framers—politicians, preachers, experts, salesman, marketers, celebrities, influencers, journalists, educators, artists—those who make their living telling the rest of us what we should look at, what we should focus on, what we should buy, what should matter.

But human beings are not the only Frames. We are not the only Framers. Our Frames are not the only Frames that influence us.

Frame This Oracle contains physical visual representations of the twenty-five Frames that shape our lives while incarnated into a physical body. These are not the sum total of all the Frames that exist (and don't exist), by any stretch of the imagination, but by using these twenty-five cards alone or . . .

1. in tandem with reading Tarot and/or other oracle decks;
2. with casting charms and other forms of divination;
3. with artwork and photographs;
4. with found objects or crystals;
5. when creating or making magic;
6. when celebrating or grieving;
7. while reading, sightseeing, or wandering;
8. during channeling or prayer or meditation; or
9. whenever you realize it's time to alter your fixed perspective and see things differently,

. . . you will gain further clarity and insight as you change your own viewpoint and focus (or glimpse the foreign viewpoints and focus of others), receiving new dimensions of meaning to accelerate your enlightenment and awakening, and discover (or remember) how mindful Framing makes for a life worth living.

WHY QUESTIONS?

One of the first things you will notice as you begin to consult the information about a specific card shared in the **Frame by Frame** section of this guidebook is that the process of asking questions is used rather than providing answers.

Too many in our modern world are seeking and relying on simple answers generated by others. When we ask questions of others, it is generally either—

a. to receive an answer outside ourselves to apply to ourselves that we hope somehow absolves us from responsibility (and/or culpability) for ourselves and our actions as well as from the resultant consequences of making a choice

—or—

b. we are asking "gotcha" questions of others to catch them in a mistake and lead them toward our preferred conclusions.

But there is another, far grander and much more vital, type of question we ask far too rarely in our modern focus on knowing and being right over learning and growth.

We discover life and how to live through questions. Children naturally start learning about the world by observing, testing, and asking, "Why?" **The more we question, the better our answers get.** Often with age and responsibilities (and lack of time), we stop questioning and settle for the known options. We get stuck in what we've decided we know. **However, the quality of our lives depends on the questions we ask. If you want to change your life, you need to change your questions.**

Questioning makes you open. It forms new patterns in the brain instead of reverting to old patterns of bias. Questioning alters our viewpoint and our consciousness, helping us realize we are the creators of our feelings and reactions; they don't just "happen" to us.

Questions reveal what you value, what you think, and who you really are. I posit that our questions reveal even more about us than our intentions, feelings, or actions! They direct and define our course through life and the world.

Questions start discussion; statements end discussion. Answers close a topic so we can move on, but questions inspire enthusiasm and hope for further exploration and unfoldment. If an answer isn't working for you, often it is because it's too simplistic and short to address the complexities and the reality of your issue. Better answers can arise only from asking better questions.

A great question directs the flow of our inquiry in expansive and illuminating ways. A poor question limits us, restricts our thinking and our choices, and lessens our options. A good question expands our thinking and options.

Those who are closest to us generally see us much more clearly than we see ourselves; if you were to ask your intimates, they would describe you more accurately than you do yourself, precisely because you are too close to yourself and have crafted far too many stories to explain why you are the way you are. Most of us need external viewpoints to help cut through our own bullshit and simply look at who we are and what we do in reality.

Questions in themselves are Frames that deliberately place distance between the self and the Watcher, so that our self, our identifications, and our consequent decisions can be viewed more lucidly and impartially. Far too often, we use answers from others or a source outside ourselves to reframe a fundamentally flawed question rather than willingly enter the void space of not-knowing that is necessary to formulate a better question.

On occasion, there will come a time when you either do not understand what a particular Frame is telling you in a reading or else you do not perceive that your question is being answered at all. Frustration can arise when we do not receive quick and easy answers to our questions, especially when we are emotionally invested in receiving a solution *now*. You might want the guidebook to clearly state what you should do; however, *Frame This Oracle* does not deliver a specific outcome: it provides a new direction. When you find yourself exasperated and out of patience, set the Frame aside and sit in the disturbing space this not-knowing creates within you. Perhaps go about your life for a time, mulling and pondering without reaching for immediate answers and comprehension. Consider the possibility that you're asking an inferior question, and use the Frame itself to devise a better question. A proper question helps us see more clearly and sparks heretofore unseen solutions to better solve our problems.

And once the right question has been asked, be prepared to sit in mental silence for a time, listening for new answers, whether they arise from yourself, the guidebook, or another source.

If I had an hour to solve a problem and my life depended on the solution, I would spend the first 55 minutes determining the proper question to ask . . . for once I know the proper question, I could solve the problem in less than five minutes.

Albert Einstein

PROPER CARE AND FEEDING OF YOUR ORACLE DECK

(WARNING: It may bite you anyway!)

Keep this deck in your purse or pocket or backpack or car, and when you are out and about . . . on a walk . . . on vacation . . . at home in your living room . . . on your front porch . . . or anywhere a person can be, use *Frame This Oracle* to focus your insight and clarify the answer you seek.

Have a simple question you need answered quickly? Find yourself wondering about the "bigger" questions? Want insight or perspective into your environment? Seeking understanding of a particular person in your life or aspect of your existence? Have you laid down a Tarot or oracle reading and need further clarification? Seeking guidance from your spirit guide or angel or otherworldly being?

Use *Frame This Oracle* to add dimensions to a Tarot or oracle reading (or both), to decipher layers of complexity that seem confusing, to focus your own insight, and to listen to your inner wisdom. Use *Frame This Oracle* to receive messages from outside sources, channeling the core of the message for greater clarity of insight.

You can choose a card at random, or you can look through the cards and choose the Frame that will focus your awareness toward the direction you need to progress. The twenty-five Frames may be further grouped into five groups of five Frames; each of these groups *Frames* a different collective viewpoint of existence:

FRAME BY FRAME

GROUP ONE LIVING

Card 1—Identity
Card 2—Love
Card 3—Alliances
Card 4—Humanity
Card 5—Life

GROUP TWO ACTIVITY

Card 6—Start
Card 7—Change
Card 8—Stop
Card 9—Image
Card 10—Reality

GROUP THREE INSPIRATION

Card 11—Physicality
Card 12—Thought
Card 13—Aesthetics
Card 14—Ethics
Card 15—Decency

GROUP FOUR ASPECT

Card 16—Individuality
Card 17—Guardians
Card 18—Provokers
Card 19—Watchers
Card 20—Divinity

GROUP FIVE MYSTERIES

Deck Back—Working with the Open Window

If you deem one Frame too limited in viewpoint or lacking the broader dimension of multiple perspectives, consider using one set of five Frames from a particular group together to garner further clarity and insight from the perspicacity of One broader Viewpoint. For example, if you have a problem you need to solve, consider utilizing the "Living" or "Activity" set. On the other hand, if you are channeling or seeking guidance of a spiritual or eternal perspective, you might use the "Aspect" or "Mysteries" set to expand your vision. If you are feeling lost and depressed, the "Inspiration" or "Mysteries" set may help. Finally, if you are unsure about the best action to take, consider working with the "Activity" or "Inspiration" set.

But choose carefully—remember that the Frames you use will alter your perception, focus, and awareness. And be ready to see what you've been missing and may not have wanted to see, presaging your prior blindness to this alien point of view.

Place your chosen Frame around the card or item you're seeking to view with greater clarity. Lay the Frame around an object in your home or that you found in nature to clarify its message for you. Conversely, if you're seeking insight into the moon, or why a particular setting affects you so profoundly (or not at all), you can hold up the Frame and look through it at your surroundings—use the Frame to separate what you wish to focus on from everything else around it. Gaze through the Frame during meditation and to focus your own psychic abilities. Place it around your scrying crystal. If channeling is your goal, write your question or message to the entity you wish to reach, or set your intention into a crystal or object, place it within the Frame, and open yourself to the incoming communication. If you wish to channel a specific Frame or understand its message more clearly, choose the Frame first and then pick up a Tarot or oracle deck, shuffle, and draw a card—placing it inside the Frame you wish to explore—to find out more about the Frame itself.

Ask yourself . . .

- What is the deeper insight this Frame reveals about the image or object it encircles?
- What is the message from this Frame for me today?
- What Frame have I been blind to?
- What further clarification or refocus do I need in order to see this issue more clearly with this Frame?
- What am I hiding from myself that needs to be revealed through this Frame?
- What wishes to speak to me through this Frame?
- What Frame do I need to focus on in this present moment?
- What Frame do I need to release, let go of, or put an end to in my life?
- What Frame do I need to embrace or welcome into my life?

Now, look up the card description in the **Frame by Frame** section of this guidebook for further direction, additional insights, and deeper understanding.

HOW TO USE *FRAME THIS ORACLE* WITH TAROT OR OTHER ORACLES

Have you ever interpreted a Tarot reading only to afterward still have essential questions that remain unanswered? Or even worse, did you find yourself with more questions after the reading than before?

One way to handle this quandary is to draw additional Tarot cards for further clarification. A more modern method is to use an oracle deck or other form of divination in tandem with the Tarot reading for greater insight.

Frame This Oracle is a vital tool created expressly for these sorts of situations. When you find yourself confused by a card reading, whether using Tarot or another oracle deck, use the Frames to

- bring focus to your reading,
- gain greater understanding of its message,
- comprehend the meaning of a particular card more fully,
- find out what you're missing in your current knowledge,
- see things from another or divergent perspective, or
- receive messages from other aspects of existence.

If you're confused by a one-card reading, simply choose a Frame and place it around the card about which you need further insight, look up the Frame's exploration in this guidebook, and use the Frame for additional clarification as to the card's message for you today.

In a multicard reading, you can either

- choose *one Frame* to delve deeper into a particular card that troubles you from the reading,

- place the *same Frame* around each card in a reading to consider that specific Frame's message for each card and the entire spread's message as a whole, or

- pick a *different Frame* for every card in the reading, placing a unique Frame around the card for which it was drawn, and interpret each individual card within the context of the distinct Frame placed around it.

Listen to your inner knowing as to which method is best for the reading you need extra illumination with in this present moment.

FRAME THIS ORACLE SPREAD IDEAS

People love to use complex cartomancy spreads in the attempt to explore all sides of an issue they are facing. I've spent many an hour myself immersed in spreads and experimenting with new ways to lay down cards in a reading.

Although these Frames can be used with any Tarot or oracle spread you prefer, let's explore some primary ways to utilize spreads with *Frame This Oracle*:

1. You can use *Frame This Oracle* with whatever Tarot or oracle spreads you prefer, using the methods outlined in the prior section of this guidebook, either by placing a Frame around one card about which you need more clarity, on or around each card in a reading, or else choosing one Frame for greater understanding of the reading in its entirety.

2. Another option is to first ask a specific question, then choose a spread that might answer your question, shuffle the Frames, lay the Frames facing downward (so that you see only the Open Window of the deck's back) in the shape of your chosen spread, and then select and place a found object or a Tarot/oracle card within each Open Window—

■ First, interpret the message of each card or object, using the **Working with the Open Window (Deck Back)** section of this guidebook.

■ Next, turn over each *Frame This Oracle* card to discover the Frame you've placed around the objects or Tarot/oracle cards. Interpret each Frame's message, using this guidebook within the greater context of your chosen spread to answer your question.

There is one more life-altering way to use *Frame This Oracle* to broaden your spiritual practice: **draw one Frame each morning to reframe your entire day.**

Drawing one Frame a day can be as valuable as regular meditation or prayer or art or writing or walks in nature.

After waking and before beginning your activities, randomly choose a Frame to carry with you throughout your day. (Alternatively, you might choose a Frame at night to guide your dreaming and focus the next day.) Read the guidebook to consider the Frame's insights and messages as well as its unique communications and perspectives. Then, go about living your day.

Occasionally, as the moment strikes you, actually hold up the card and view whatever you are looking at through this day's Frame, pausing to consider the Frame's insights into what you are seeing and experiencing. Allow the Frame to draw your attention to details you might have otherwise overlooked, and expand your perspective to consider alternate possibilities you may be missing.

And no, you do not have to hold up the Frame physically. If you feel it's time for a reframing but you're in a situation wherein it would be awkward to hold up a card (although I suggest that doing so might prompt a profound communication with those around you that you don't want to miss!), simply mentally envision the Frame around what you need to see more clearly in order to alter your current focus; you can even make a square with your thumbs and forefingers for a quick makeshift frame if you prefer.

As your day draws to a close, contemplate all the insights gleaned from your Frame of the day, perhaps writing down, meditating on, or praying about what you've realized.

One Frame a day forces you to regularly get out of your own (habitual) viewpoint, be more open to and even channel other perspectives, and change your focus so you can see *what is* at this moment (rather than what it's always been, what you think it is, or what you think it should be).

Alternatively, you could pull one Tarot or oracle card a day from your favorite deck and place one Frame around it. Interpret this combination and then carry both cards around throughout your day, viewing the world through their joint communication—or take a photograph of the combo with your cell phone to bring with you effortlessly!

A FEW WORDS ON CHANNELING

Channeling is a challenging idea for some people. Skeptics aside, the very idea of opening oneself up to being influenced or even, in a deep trance, controlled by an external source can be an alarming proposition indeed. How can we know we are safe? How can we trust both the person doing the channeling and the entity being channeled? Even assuming the best of intentions and honesty of all involved, just how reliable can the messages received via channeling be, really?

A "channel" is a conduit that directs the flow of something from one source to another—a stream, agent, mouthpiece, instrument, intermediary, vehicle, tool, or medium of transference.

Each of the Frames found in *Frame This Oracle* is by this definition a channel.

Sometimes these Frames will channel an entity that you recognize or feels familiar to you. It's possible to use the Frames to develop relationships with these entities as your guides, but not necessary or required in any way. In fact, at times, doing so would be ill advised.

These Frames can also channel a communication about the future, if you're open. Many spirits view us embodied beings from a broader lens with regard to time. We are as much spirits as they and thus exist (from their perspective) outside space and time, where the past, present, and future exist simultaneously. However, these beings are individual entities with their own experiences and personalities; channeling with *Frame This Oracle* uncovers the information that the entities being channeled deem relevant, as opposed to answering your question in the Delphic oracular tradition.

And it is critical to note that it is quite possible these entities may lie, either to deliberately deceive you or unintentionally misleading you as they communicate something they believe to be so that is actually incorrect.

People who are uncomfortable or confused by the very idea of channeling might find it helpful, before using the Frames, to spend a quiet, thoughtful moment attuning to that part of themselves that is always connected to the Source or All That Is. Some call it "raising our vibration," but it is simply developing a quiet, peaceful mind. The key to receptivity is development of inner stillness and connection with higher self. Essence at ease. Opening. Let go of any expectations or fear. We release any illusions, desires, or dreams we've been carrying, making space for a new quality of stillness and acceptance of what is, an ability to welcome the new that is outside our presuppositions and preconceptions. We slow down and acknowledge the connection we've always had. Be at ease in this new reality that always was.

Many associate channeling with a trance or altered state of consciousness. The Frames can be used to access these transformative states, but it is in no way necessary or even preferable. The Frames are intended to provide a tool for everyone to receive messages with full consciousness.

Experienced channelers speak of traveling through a doorway or portal to reach the spirit world—let each Frame be your personal doorway to alternate viewpoints, communications, sources, and dimensions. When using the Frames to channel, some might find that chanting, singing, humming, or any sonorous intonation helps focus the attention and raise one's vibrational state. However, it's a mistake to assume that these channeled messages are far away or difficult to reach—it's only our own limiting beliefs, shortsighted denials, and focus on material concerns that prevent us from receiving these messages all the time.

If a communication comes through that seems negative, dark, scary, or dangerous, it's vital to acknowledge the communication but then banish the sender from your presence, breaking the connection and closing the gateway. The Frames put you in the driver's seat, enabling you to stop any connection, continuing association only with those beings with whom you wish. You can receive and acknowledge another's or others' communications without going into agreement or resonating with it or them. Never accept another's or others' communication as substitute for your own looking and knowing, for this can initiate the dark road to oppression and even possession. Parasitic entities can prey on you as an energy source only if you invite them; exercise your sovereign right to say no.

Further shield yourself by asking for protection, stating your clear intention, and banishing anything that you do not wish to stay connected with. Call upon Source or guardians for safety, use a magical circle, perform a banishment ritual, say a prayer, radiate positive energy and white light, or implement your preferred spiritual practice to dispel unwanted energies from your presence. I've even found that telling jokes and laughing, especially with those you love and who love you back, can do wonders for shattering any lasting vestiges of negative influence.

Also be mindful of what in you resonated with this unwanted entity that forged the connection. Sometimes they come with a strong message that some part of you desires to hear, sometimes you need to be more precise with a clear intention to receive specific answers, and sometimes you don't wish to connect with them because of a truth about yourself

35

that resonates with them, which you don't want to see or acknowledge.

You must be able to discern between your own thought and a message or impression from another being. A good hint is that a channeled message cannot be changed because it did not originate from you; you cannot simply change your mind about it. You can disagree, but a channeled communication feels more like a command. Instead of thinking, "I wonder if I need to change something . . . ," you will clearly receive a message: "Change *this.*"

Channeling is not a passive act; it's a cooperative process. Sometimes you will use a Frame and it will seem as though divinity slapped you across the face to point your eyes toward a message. Other times you will barely receive the slightest hint that there is something that needs to shift. It works best to acknowledge the Frame's communication, no matter how subtle.

Integrating all twenty-five Frames into your life can eventually become like breathing. Just as our breath is a constant reminder of the Source that joins All That Is, guiding and sustaining all of us continuously in the flow of existence, so acknowledging and receiving the communications of these twenty-five Frames echoes the breath of life that fills and surrounds being as both action and impetus.

Some possible ways to use the Frames when channeling include

- automatic writing or drawing,
- creative muse for making art,
- refocus of attention toward alternate aspects of existence, and
- point of focus to enter meditative state or trance.

Just remember, the method is your choice and always in your control.

A traditional approach to channeling that may be used with *Frame This Oracle* might follow this ritual pattern:

- Breathe, relax, and center your mind.

- Connect the mind/body with your preferred method of resonance.

- Choose and place your Frame as portal.

- Receive the entire communication.

- Give thanks.

- Return by putting away the Frame and grounding yourself in the here and now. (I prefer bubble baths and hot tea.)

Alternatively, you might choose the Frame for the source you wish to hear a message from—either intentionally or at random—and explore one of these approaches:

- Place the Frame on a blank piece of paper and inside draw/doodle/write whatever words/phrases/images arise for you.

- Meditate and listen as you focus on the Frame to receive the message for you from that particular source. Stay open to receive a specific communication as to what needs to be placed within the Frame, find and place this object/image/backdrop, and continue to meditate and listen with this refocused attention.

- Draw a Tarot or oracle card *after* initially working with your chosen Frame alone, place in the center of the Frame, and receive the additional message that aspect of existence wishes to tell you.

One final caveat: One of the biggest problems in life that the majority of people are oblivious to is unacknowledged communication that originates from someone other than oneself.

Most human beings are virtually unaware of the problems created for themselves and existence itself as a result of unacknowledged communication. Over time, these unacknowledged messages pile up around and within us, building mass as we continue to refuse to receive them, eventually creating a mess of reality and our ability to perceive it. Communications that remain sufficiently unacknowledged will increasingly manifest in the circumstances surrounding us.

When encountering such communications, remember: *Acknowledgment is not agreement.* You can receive and acknowledge a communication without going into agreement with it or accepting it as true. I can listen to and acknowledge your assertion that there is a cat in the room without agreeing or pretending I see a cat when I do not.

There are nine ways that a message can flow from one source to another:

1. from you to yourself
2. from you to someone else
3. from someone else to you
4. from someone else back to themselves
5. from someone else to someone else
6. rom someone else to a group of others
7. from a group to itself
8. from a group to someone else
9. from one group to another group

If you suspect that you, your space, and your self-sovereignty might be getting mucked up by unacknowledged communications, I suggest using each of the twenty-five Frames to clean up this confusion for yourself. This task seems daunting at the outset (especially if you've knowingly rejected communications out of fear, anger, or distaste), but on the other side of acknowledging all the communications you've ignored or rejected, life becomes remarkably free and open for a being.

One aspect of each Frame in *Frame This Oracle* is to receive a message from a particular source—the Frame tells you the source who wishes to communicate with you, and the message that needs to be received or acknowledged (or both) is contained within the Frame.

To clean up unacknowledged communications for yourself with a given Frame, after placing a Frame around something, ask yourself these questions:

- What communication needs to be acknowledged?
- From what source would this be a desired (or undesired) communication?
- What is this source telling me through this Frame?
- What unacknowledged message is Framed here?

I repeat, you are only receiving and acknowledging the message, not necessarily agreeing with it. Each of these twenty-five Frames offers you a method to channel communications from sources other than yourself that, prior to working with these Frames, you might not even have realized were communicating with you!

FRAME BY FRAME

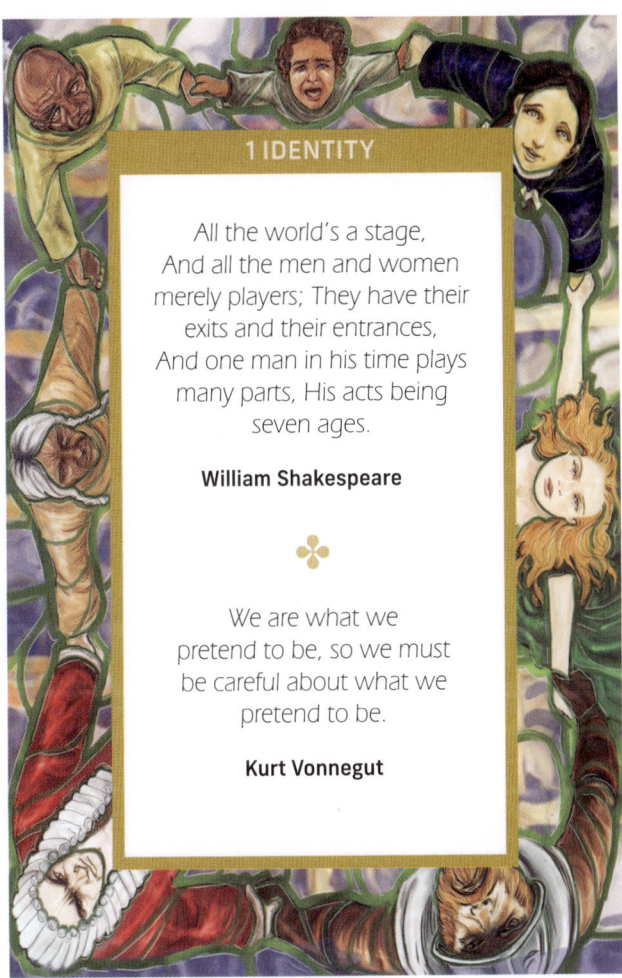

All the world's a stage,
And all the men and women
merely players; They have their
exits and their entrances,
And one man in his time plays
many parts, His acts being
seven ages.

William Shakespeare

❖

We are what we
pretend to be, so we must
be careful about what we
pretend to be.

Kurt Vonnegut

IDENTITY

The **Identity** Frame is those aspects of existence with which you've identified yourself. It indicates what you've decided you are as opposed to what you've decided you are not, what you're actively reiterating to structure your present beingness. Of course, both what "you are" and what "you are not" are choices and decisions (and lies, or—if you prefer—make-believe) of separation you're telling yourself to establish a personality, a persona, an ego, and—you guessed it—your **Identity.**

The **Identity** is those aspects of you that are fleeting, passing, changing, malleable, mortal, formative, substantial, material, physical, and influenced by environment as well as others and will one day cease when your heart stops beating.

Identity is who you (and those around you) believe you are in this lifetime of human experience. That which you are afraid will disappear when you die.

Ask yourself . . .

■ Look into the **Identity** Frame to see the message from and for this particular lifetime you are living, as defined by this specific time and space you are occupying in this moment. How does the fleeting nature of **Identity** make this message all the more precious? Are you content with your present identifications, or is it time to identify with or as something else?

■ What particular stage of life or part are you playing in your life to establish, define, and distinguish yourself from the rest (e.g., youth, parent, adult, hero, seeker, middle age, rebel, worker, player, lover, elder, expert)? Is this focus serving you? Within the **Identity** Frame, find your answer.

■ What do the contents of the **Identity** Frame indicate you are pretending is eternal and "really you" that is, in fact, transitory and mortal?

■ What lies, fantasies, and longings do you see revealed in the **Identity** Frame that you are being as "you" and telling yourself in order to live and believe the story you've decided is you, your life, and this lifetime?

■ What you've placed within the **Identity** Frame asks you to consider where you have come from and what you are becoming. Is there solace or a warning in this?

■ Does what you've placed within the **Identity** Frame reveal hidden aspects and consequences of your present stage in the cycle of life and living that you have been ignoring or abandoning, maybe even to excessive and destructive ends? Gaze into the **Identity** Frame for guidance and clarity.

■ What is the message your present **Identity** needs to hear . . . say . . . uncover . . . or unlock? Within the **Identity** Frame, find the key.

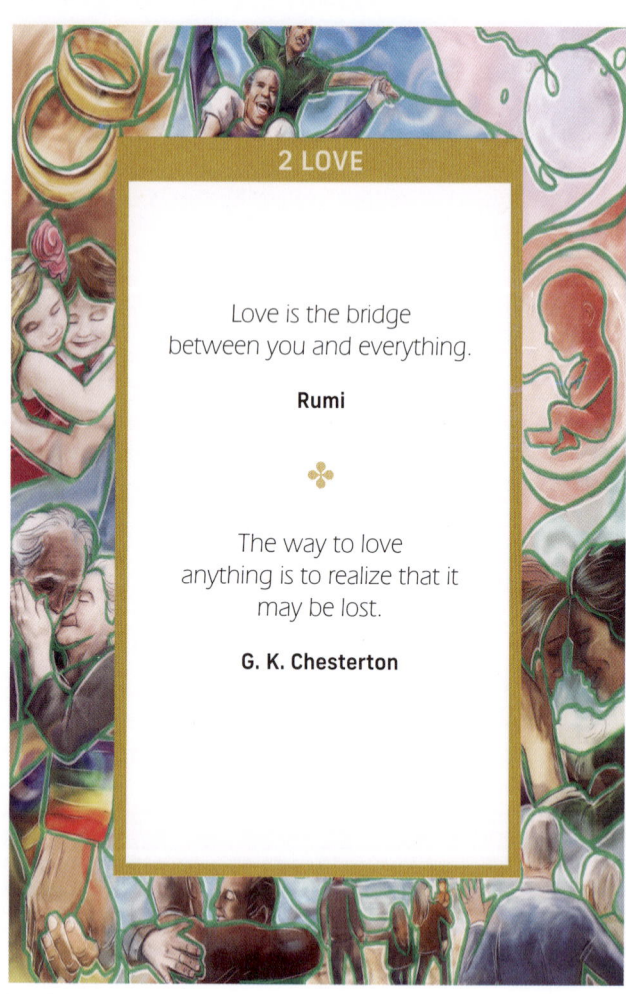

2 LOVE

Love is the bridge
between you and everything.

Rumi

The way to love
anything is to realize that it
may be lost.

G. K. Chesterton

LOVE

The Frame of **Love** is the force that brings us together to join, merge, mate, unite, and make more out of two (or many). We lose our separation in **Love**'s ecstasy and agony of fusion, that process of contraction (as opposed to the expansion of Frame Five: Life) that powers the sun and the stars as well as creates new life.

Love pulls us all together, dissolving our divisions, melting our defenses, and unifying our opposites. **Love** encompasses romance, sex, and family, of course, but also any intimate relationship. **Love** is that influence that makes us get along . . . helps us resolve conflict . . . draws us closer . . . binds us mutually . . . that familiarity we experience when we see who we are, what we believe, what we think, and what we feel reflected in another's experience. **Love** makes us larger than ourselves.

Of course, in **Love** we can lose ourselves entirely. **Love** can be a dangerous and destructive pressure, urge, compulsion, and craving to be reckoned with, deeply satisfying in its fulfillment but crushing when in excess. Its absence makes us feel alone, hopeless, obsessed, divided, cut off, lacking, insufficient, and small.

Ask yourself . . .

■ What do the contents of the **Love** Frame suggest you need to see about the intimate relationships in your life? Do you have a message to yourself about **Love**? Contrariwise, does what you've placed within the **Love** Frame suggest you're focusing on **Love** to the detriment of some other aspect of life and living?

■   Often the **Love** Frame will show you how **Love** is manifesting in your life today. Is it helping you or harming you? Do you need to change something, or is it time to deepen your investment?

■   Sometimes what you find inside the **Love** Frame will reveal how your own actions are affecting your **Love** relationships. Is your **Love** and its expression beneficial or toxic to those you seek to **Love**? Is it time to examine how you show others that you love them?

■   How do you receive **Love**? How do you give **Love**? Are these methods working for you? What can you change to experience more satisfying **Love** relationships? Look into the **Love** Frame for guidance.

■   What message do you see within the **Love** frame about sex and your sexuality today?

■   How are your past family, romantic, sexual, and **Love** relationships influencing your present? What do you need to address, release, confront, or forgive in order to move on? Your clues lie within the **Love** Frame.

■   The **Love** Frame might ask who your family is and how they are impacting your life. Is the person you're being in your family relationships the person you wish to be? If your family continues as it is today, is it the best direction for all involved, or does something need to change? Within the **Love** frame lies your direction.

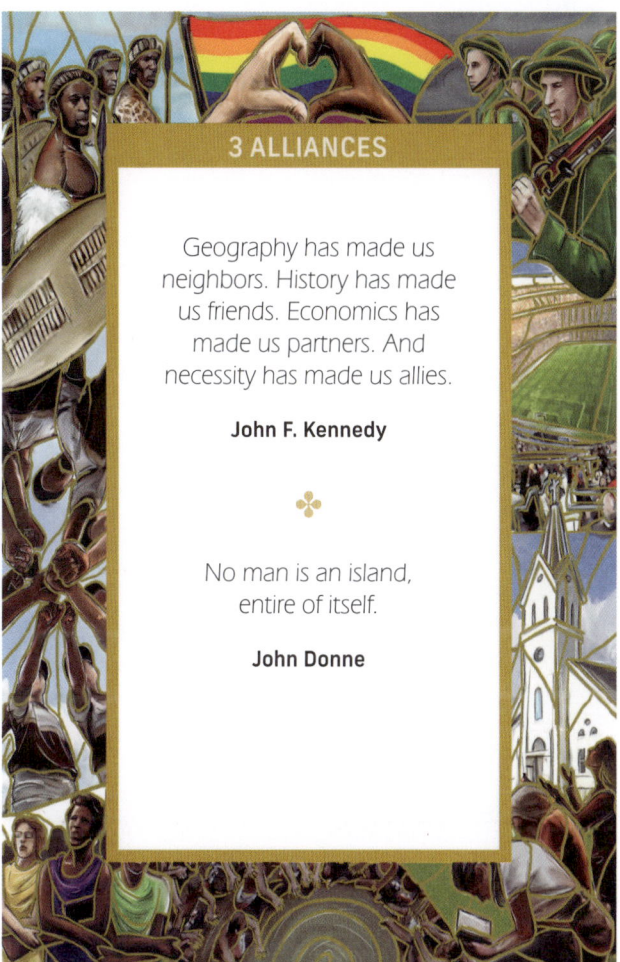

3 ALLIANCES

Geography has made us neighbors. History has made us friends. Economics has made us partners. And necessity has made us allies.

John F. Kennedy

❖

No man is an island, entire of itself.

John Donne

ALLIANCES

The Frame of **Alliances** discusses the groups we are a part of as opposed to those of which we are not a part. Who is for us and who is against us? Who are our allies and who are our enemies? Who is inside and who is outside? Whom do we welcome and whom do we reject? With whom do we feel safe and whom do we deem dangerous? Who are our people / like us / inner circle / our clan / in-group and who are alien / other / different / strangers / out-group?

Alliances are the groups and systems we are a part of for security, identity, passion, and strength. They are based on shared agreements (or shared disagreements). Just because someone else might associate you with a particular group does not mean this group is one of your **Alliances**. In order for a group to be an **Alliance**, you must ally or identify yourself with the group.

An **Alliance** can be formed by two people or millions. Some **Alliances** are consciously chosen, while others are assumed at birth or consented to through community. **Alliances** have the potential both to improve and ruin our lives and our experience of living. They restrict us, compel us, shape us, inspire us, protect us, and develop us. Human beings are social creatures, and your **Alliances** reveal your identity as derived from your groups.

Ask yourself . . .

■ Look into the **Alliances** Frame to see your present **Alliances** reflected. Are they serving or impeding you? Do they help you become the person you wish to be? Is it time to make a change or else acknowledge and be grateful for particular

Alliances? Do you speak as your **Alliances** rather than as yourself**?**

■ The **Alliances** Frame indicates a direct transmission from one of the **Alliances** you've made. Do you accept or reject this communication? Do you like the person you are becoming if you accept/believe/follow this message? Do you agree with the reality your **Alliance** is creating by accepting/believing/following this idea?

■ Is there a hidden message or communication that you need to receive from one of your **Alliances** revealed within the **Alliances** Frame? Inversely, is one of your **Alliances** hiding a critical truth about itself from you? Do you have a message to yourself about your **Alliances**?

■ Do you like the person your **Alliances** are shaping you to be? Ponder what the contents of the **Alliances** Frame say about who you are and what you're becoming under the sway of your **Alliances.**

■ It's time to consider what forms the foundation of your **Alliances**—why are you a part of the groups that you identify with? What do you share? Are your **Alliances** based on camaraderie, love, fear, hate, exclusion, survival, need, identity, anger, enthusiasm, ideals, opportunities, retaliation, belonging, or something else? Does membership in your groups serve the person you are becoming? Within the **Alliances** Frame, find these answers.

■ Consider your personal identification within the following common human **Alliances**: family, friends, municipality, nation, political party, clubs or hobbies, education, work, sports, social media groups, religious or spiritual affiliations, ethnic or cultural alliances, social ideologies, etc. Are you glad you have allied yourself with these groups? Why or why not? What do you see inside the **Alliances** Frame to give you further insights? Do you want to leave, find a new group, or become more actively involved?

■ Does the **Alliance** Frame reveal that an **Alliance** you are not a part of has a message for you? What is this other **Alliance's** communication?

Alliances have the potential both to improve and ruin our lives and our experience of living … your Alliances reveal your identity as derived from your groups.

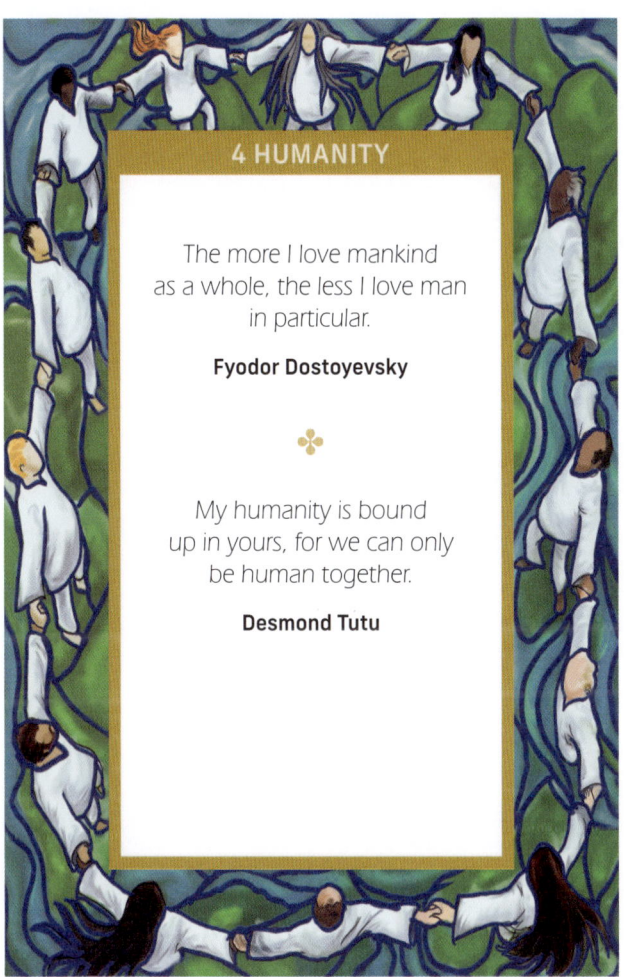

4 HUMANITY

The more I love mankind
as a whole, the less I love man
in particular.

Fyodor Dostoyevsky

❖

My humanity is bound
up in yours, for we can only
be human together.

Desmond Tutu

HUMANITY

This Frame indicates messages to or from the collective human race as a whole. These communications can originate from **Humanity**'s past, present, future, or from the world of **Humanity**'s wishes, ideals, should bes, and not to bes.

When the **Humanity** Frame is pulled, get ready for a mind-blowing perspective that is life altering in its broader implications both for the individual and the collective together. Survival of the *Homo sapiens* species, its evolution and progress, lessons that must be learned (often or else), and predictions concerning repercussions for our public actions, as well as the convergence of our private choices on the worldwide stage, will be revealed.

Humanity may also address what it is that makes us human in contrast to other species and beings, both physical and discarnate. What does it really mean to be human? To truly grasp **Humanity**'s considerations, you must think of yourself as one cell in a vast array of cells that make up one body, that body being the genetic entity we call **Humanity**.

Ask yourself . . .

■ What does **Humanity** wish to communicate to you through its Frame today? Do you have a message to yourself about **Humanity**?

■ What does the **Humanity** Frame suggest you need to see about **Humanity** that you're blind to? What are you fixated on about **Humanity**? What do you need to let go of with regard to **Humanity**?

■ Are you more human, inhuman, nonhuman, or superhuman? Does your **Humanity** satisfy or disappoint you? How at home do you feel as part of the human race? What do the contents of the **Humanity** Frame say about this?

■ What do you need to confront about **Humanity**'s past in order to understand what is Framed? Do you play a part in this piece of **Humanity**'s history? Do you need to release, accept, or move on as a result of this revelation?

■ What do you need to accept about **Humanity**'s future in order to realize what is Framed? How does this future affect you? Can you play a part in accomplishing or avoiding this outcome?

■ What do you embrace about **Humanity**? What are you avoiding about **Humanity**? What do you agree with **Humanity** about? What do you disagree with **Humanity** about? What do you like about being human? What do you dislike about being human? What does the **Humanity** Frame reveal to you about your affinity (or lack thereof) with **Humanity**?

■ Do the contents of the **Humanity** Frame suggest harm or help? How are you harming **Humanity**? How are you helping **Humanity**? How does **Humanity** harm you? How does **Humanity** help you?

Life is not a problem
to be solved, but a reality to
be experienced.

Søren Kierkegaard

❦

Many people are alive
but don't touch the miracle
of being alive.

Thich Nhat Hanh

LIFE

The **Life** Frame suggests a communication to you from **Life** itself. **Life** comprises all living beings in existence—with the capacity for growth, metabolism, reproduction, and response to change—as a collective entity. If it can die, it is a part of **Life**.

Whereas Love (see Frame Two) is the process of fusion and contraction, **Life** is the process of division and expansion. **Life** separates existence into ever more complex evolving forms of distinctive characteristics, expanding the breadth and potential of existence. **Life's** impetus is division—although more-complex life forms reproduce by fusion initially, the very cells that compose them reproduce through mitosis, or multiple fission.

Messages via this Frame often originate from all living organisms as a group, but a communication might also materialize from **Life** itself as a force, direction, or energy. **Life** is the power that separates, expands, grows, differentiates, evolves, expresses, procreates, transforms, functions, increases, destroys, challenges, rises, overcomes, and competes to survive and persist. **Life** *becomes*. As Dr. Ian Malcolm says in the iconic film *Jurassic Park*, "**Life** finds a way."

Ask yourself . . .

■ What does **Life** wish to communicate to you today via its Frame? Is there something you need to tell yourself about **Life**? Is there a specific aspect or entity of **Life** that needs to speak to you?

■ What do the contents of the **Life** Frame suggest you need to see about **Life** that you might be missing? What are you preoccupied with concerning **Life** and living? What do you need to release with regard to **Life**? What do you need to embrace about **Life**?

■ Is the **Life** Frame asking you to think about your experience of **Life** and living? Are you content to be alive? Why are you alive? Do you recognize your bond with **Life** and all living things or feel the outsider?

■ The **Life** Frame reminds you to live your life more organically. Is your day-to-day existence too separated from **Life**? Are you spending too much time in the manufactured world of concrete and cubicles or the virtual world of cyberspace and social media? Is it time to retreat to the wild, natural world for a time, where **Life** is more visceral and unscripted?

■ How in tune are you with your **Life** as a biological being, both singly and as a part of the grander biosphere? Consider the rhythms and cycles of your days, months, and years, as well as the state of your health in light of what the contents of the **Life** Frame show you. Do you live your **Life** in a state of balance and well-being, or are you disordered and unbalanced?

■ What do you see within the **Life** Frame about **Life's** terrible realities? Are you in denial of the darker sides of **Life**? **Life** consumes and destroys to persist. **Life** is hard, unjust, and painful. All **Life** ends. Conversely, are these harsher realities all you perceive about **Life**? Are you missing the glory and abundance of this gift we call **Life**?

■ Where are you in your own **Life** cycle right now? What does the **Life** Frame show you that you need to accept about your **Life?** What does it suggest you change about your present stage of **Life** to live more fully?

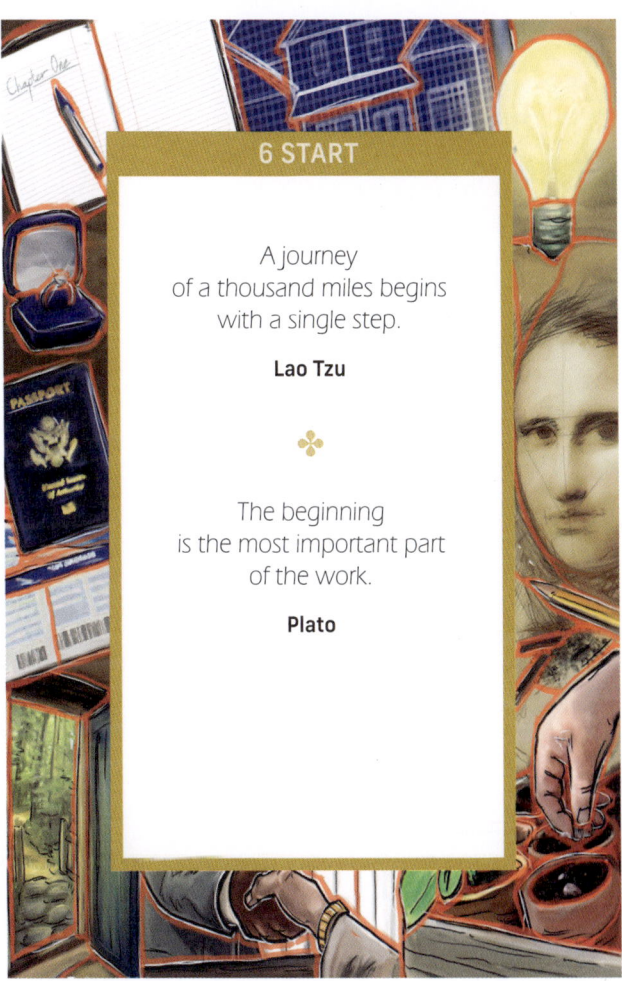

A journey
of a thousand miles begins
with a single step.

Lao Tzu

❖

The beginning
is the most important part
of the work.

Plato

START

The **Start** Frame represents the point in time or space in which something has its origin—the inception of a new (and, it's hoped, better) path, the birth, the inciting incident, the launch—whether by choice, catalyst, or chance. **Start** indicates anything new in our lives. **Start**ing ignites us with vital passion, hope, and potential possibilities.

A **Start** is the beginning of a cycle of action—the scattering, dispersal, or release of energy in all directions (or a particular aim) that sets everything in motion.

Ask yourself . . .

■ What do you need to **Start**? Are you unsure, afraid, or procrastinating? Why are you hesitating? Look inside the **Start** Frame to explore this new direction and find the encouragement you need to get **Start**ed.

■ The **Start** Frame can suggest new insights into handling the surmounting problems you're facing with **Start**ing something. What are the issues and barriers? Look to the contents of the **Start** Frame to see the way through.

■ Have you or another **Start**ed something that you now regret? Are you carrying the emotional baggage of pain or even trauma about past disastrous **Start**s that is preventing you from beginning something new today? Consider the contents of the **Start** Frame to point you toward the answer you seek about this dilemma and **Start** the process of forgiveness and recovery.

■ Sometimes the **Start** Frame points out the need to look at something from a new perspective—to **Start** a project fresh, to turn a topic upside down or inside out. Lighten up, loosen your control, and expand your narrow vision. Is it time to shake things up and allow the energy to disperse more freely and in all directions for a time to **Start** something better?

■ Do you constantly **Start** new things but struggle to finish? What is so exciting about the new and distasteful about the old? Do you romanticize beginnings and the new, always hoping the next great adventure or fix is being started now or is just over the next horizon? It's easy to idealize the **Start** of something when its finale is far distant, but when we're in the midst of it we see the obstacles, often getting overwhelmed and quitting. New ideas are easy, but it's in the execution and realization that challenges arise. Do you need to be grateful for what you have, and focus on the good in your life rather than using fresh **Start**s to avoid what is or is not? What does the **Start** Frame indicate you need to think about practically in order to move forward?

■ The contents of the **Start** Frame can guide your attention to something **Start**ing around you that you might be missing. Is your present understanding of the external world and your own internal order making you blind to something that is **Start**ing or what might be? Are you too decided, or do you know too much about what you've resolved is so, to perceive a prospective opportunity **Start**ing?

■ Within this Frame is the inspiration you need for a successful **Start**. Use this wisdom to reframe your direction to sharpen your focus and momentum.

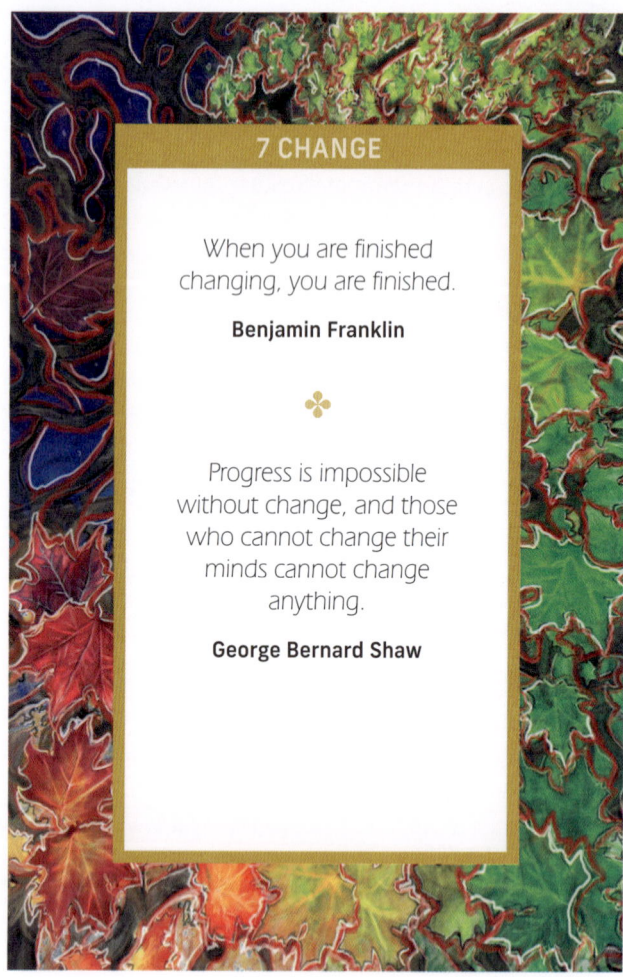

When you are finished changing, you are finished.

Benjamin Franklin

♣

Progress is impossible without change, and those who cannot change their minds cannot change anything.

George Bernard Shaw

CHANGE

A **Change** is a directed flow of movement or action toward a different trajectory. Alteration, improvement, adjustment, transformation, amendment, growth, progression, and adaptation, but also regression, decay, conversion, retreat, decline, perversion, sabotage, and contamination. Some people love **Change** so much they sloganize it; others fear **Change** as the enemy of The Way Things Are. **Change** makes a fixed condition unstable, and so many would prefer to remain stuck (and feel secure). People by and large welcome **Change** if we initiate it, but loathe any **Change** forced upon us.

Most of what we see happening in the physical universe is **Change**, for **Change** is what makes things persist. Things that do not change, die. Heraclitus observed this when he said, "The only constant in life is change." Many of us love starting but **Change** only in order to postpone the inevitable ending.

Ask yourself . . .

■ What do you need to **Change**? Look to the contents of the **Change** Frame to find out.

■ Is there a **Change** that is happening around you or needs to happen, but you're blind to it or unable to embrace it because of your decision to keep things as they are? Are your beliefs about yourself, others, or reality getting in the way of seeing **Change** clearly? Consider the contents of the **Change** Frame to understand what you're missing in your determination to avoid **Change.**

■ **Change** often challenges us to consider the subject of control in our lives: Who has it? Who wants it? Who's abdicating it? What **Change** needs to be made to maintain or obtain control? Perhaps you find yourself out of control—of yourself or the situation. Are you vilifying control itself or rejecting your responsibility for **Change**? The **Change** Frame dares you to regain your capacity for control: Are you equally able to create something new, **Change** the existing order, and stop something when it no longer serves you or its purpose? You must be able to do all three to maintain control. Inside the **Change** Frame, find your way to get control.

■ Have your survival needs been threatened, paralyzing you into believing no **Change** is possible? Do you see the need for **Change** but have no idea how to accomplish it? Inside the **Change** Frame, discover the answer to your quandary.

■ Often, our issues about **Change** are mixed up with our disagreements with time and timing, for **Change** is the primary manifestation of time. What bothers you about time and its influence in your life or the lives of those whom you care about? Is there a natural or external **Change** happening that you don't like or believe is ill timed? Do you oppose an impending **Change**? The **Change** Frame contains the way through your problem with time and the **Change** that bothers you so.

■ Is something troubling you about a lasting condition? Do you find yourself unable to see the way to **Change** something you know needs changing? Sometimes the **Change** Frame shows you the truth that needs to be exposed or the lie you must fully acknowledge in order to move on. The more lies we tell ourselves and others, the less likely we are to be able to successfully **Change** a worsening situation, for we must recognize what a thing is before we can hope to successfully **Change** it for the better.

■ Be prepared to confront a problem displayed within the **Change** Frame that you are desperately trying to **Change** in order to prevent something ending. How many times has this been **Change**d in the attempt to keep it going? What (if anything) remains that was originally intended? If the problem seems unsolvable, you need to take a step back and dismantle your personal disagreements, denials, and lies that blind you to seeing the situation clearly. Allow the message within the **Change** Frame to evoke options and answers to help you find acceptance and relief.

Change is what makes things persist. Things that do not change, die.

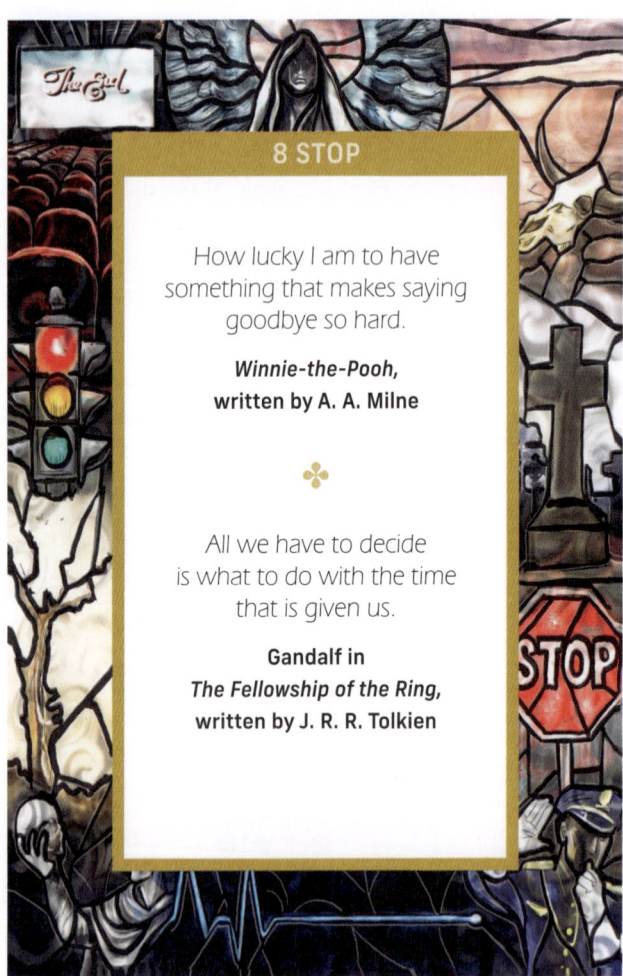

How lucky I am to have
something that makes saying
goodbye so hard.

Winnie-the-Pooh,
written by A. A. Milne

❦

All we have to decide
is what to do with the time
that is given us.

Gandalf in
The Fellowship of the Ring,
written by J. R. R. Tolkien

STOP

To **Stop** is to cease activity or come to an end. Many of us hate endings—especially those out of our control. However, the natural cycle of activity in the physical universe is *Start—Change—***Stop**, with **Stop** being an equally essential component to every cycle. Too much of any one portion of the cycle, and we get restless, longing for the others. Starting can be daunting and exhausting . . . changing can be tedious and unsettling. Pain is a sign that something isn't working, and things must **Stop** not only to make way for the new, but because life's rhythms are finite and limited.

Most of us tend to prefer some activities over others. Some love everything new; they're all about potential, excitement, invention, ingenuity. Others love changing things—improving, correcting, fine-tuning, perfecting. There are even a portion of us that prefer **Stop**ping things—for control or dominance, sure, but also to put an end to what's deemed harmful and evil, granting relief from a progressively worsening sequence of corruption and decay.

But the physical universe isn't simply cyclical. The narrower our outlook, the more we perceive changes as **Stop**s, for just as everything in the physical universe is both a particle and a wave, so every perceived cycle is simultaneously but a portion of a broader spiral: it's only from our own vantage point upon a particular curve we . . . cannot . . . quite . . . see . . . beyond that we experience more **Stop** than start, more **Stop** than change.

Everything that starts will one day **Stop**; often, it is only when we humans become aware that our experience of something or someone is limited—that it will **Stop**—that we begin to appreciate it. Our bounded embodied identities need the perspective of endings to value what is ours right now.

Only what will one day **Stop** dreads ending; only what is in danger of being **Stop**ped worries about **Stop**ping. All things of the physical universe **Stop**, even the physical universe itself. The eternal part of us—that part that does not **Stop**—does not fear endings, because the cycles of activity neither start, change, nor **Stop** its essence, for it is not of this world.

Ask yourself . . .

■ Gaze into the Frame to see what needs to **Stop**. If you're unsure, a good place to start is by asking, "Where is the pain?" Do you find yourself confronting friction or opposition? Are you feeling blocked in some way? No matter what you do, does it seem as though you're trapped within a cycle of failure? These are signs it's time for something to end.

■ Are you being **Stop**ped? Do you need to be **Stop**ped? Is this **Stop**ping a help or a hindrance, and to whom? Look to the contents of the **Stop** Frame to find out if **Stop**ping is the problem or if your reaction to **Stop**ping is the issue.

■ The **Stop** Frame may be warning you about something you've **Stop**ped: Is it time to reexamine a decision you've made or conclusion you've come to that's no longer serving you? Have things changed, and now you're missing something crucial in your dedication to this way you've ordered your present reality? Do the contents of the **Stop** Frame confuse or disturb you because they suggest something you thought improbable or even impossible on the basis of your present understanding? Is it time to **Stop Stop**ping yourself?

■ Sometimes the **Stop** Frame suggests you're **Stopping** something before its time. Is your first reaction to something new a negative one? Have you been trying to **Stop** everyone and everything around you? Why? Are you bothered by another, challenged by their freedom of expression in ways you've **Stop**ped yourself? It's time to examine this unbridled **Stop**ping, since too much **Stop**ping leads to a destructive or even destroyed life.

■ On the other hand, are you unwilling to **Stop**? Do you feel that things must not **Stop** so you can deal with "the way things are" and feel okay? Do you believe that society is broken, life is merely suffering, freedom is a lie, or love brings only misery? The contents of the **Stop** Frame point the way through such hopeless **Stop**ping.

■ Have you lost the ability to **Stop** things? Do you believe that things are un**Stop**pable? The abilities to decide, choose, conclude, and believe are all examples of utilizing the capacity to **Stop**. The contents of the **Stop** Frame suggest what you need to **Stop** to order your confusion and regain sovereignty of yourself.

■ Be prepared for what's inside the **Stop** Frame to expose your unacknowledged sorrow—grief for what you've lost, what you fear losing, or what is ending. We are told that nothing ever truly ends, but ofttimes these seem but empty words: the small, the passing, the unique never truly recurs exactly as it was. Thus, we mourn the **Stop**ping of what will never be again . . . its unique identity to us . . . what we have identified with. It is fear of losing identity—what we have identified with in this physical lifetime and the identity we've formed during embodiment—that **Stop** suggests we must first recognize and at last let go.

67

There are always
two people in every picture:
the photographer and
the viewer.

Ansel Adams

❖

The map is not the
territory; the word is not the
thing it describes.

Alfred Korzybski

IMAGE

An **Image** is a representation or conception reflecting something that depicts our experience of the thing (as opposed to the actual thing itself). The senses of the body perceive phenomena and form **Image**s to explain, classify, interpret, and remember them. Henceforth, it is not what *actually occurred* that we remember, but our partial and developed internal **Image**s merged with understandings, decisions, beliefs, and attitudes about the lived phenomenon, for our memories do not separate the things from ourselves.

Experience itself is nothing but separate sensations, yet we are not passive cameras equally recording all we encounter. We pick and choose what we perceive from the myriad sensations, forming them into ideas, transforming their chaos into the **Image**s that make up our internal order. **Image**s are created as we sense unorganized stimuli, receive these sensations through the ordered lens of our own perceptions, and finally conceive our **Image**s through organizing these perceptions. The world as we know it is a construction as opposed to reality: we know nothing but our manner of perceiving sensations and the **Image**s we conceive as we experience them.

Images are thus our internal identity merged with our *perceptions* of our external reality. In each **Image** we insert a bit of our self, our identity right now, and it becomes a part of us (or a not-part of us). Our **Image**s are inextricably melded with our identity and ever changing—as we tell ourselves stories about each **Image** again and again, so too the **Image** morphs with our emergent identity throughout our lives. The **Image** Frame reveals what we've decided we need things to be, in contrast to what they are (or were or will be).

Ask yourself . . .

■ What do the contents of the **Image** Frame reveal about your *idea* regarding the subject under consideration as opposed to the *actuality*? Are your internal order and understanding altering or misperceiving the actuality in some way? How does the **Image** reflect you and not the thing itself?

■ Is there an **Image** (or **Images**) shown within the **Image** Frame created by someone else that you've used to order your internal reality and explain the way things are in the world? Is this source trustworthy or skewed? Is it time to look anew, reevaluate, and craft your own **Image** to interact with what you perceive to be so? How might this **Image** reflect the person or group communicating it?

■ Is there an ancient **Image** that speaks to you throughout time—calling you to explore the truths and ramifications suggested by its message? Gaze into the contents of the **Image** Frame to discover and explore this **Image** and its meaning for your life today.

■ Are you sensing something but not acknowledging it? Is there an experience you've had or are having that's been denied, ignored, maligned, or lied about? Perhaps the contents of the **Image** Frame are displaying aspects of reality that you need to see more fully in order to move forward.

■ Often, our **Image**s are not based on what things are, but what we feel things should be—what we want or need them to be. How does what's within the **Image** Frame protect your present identity? Might you be using this **Image** to preserve your beliefs about life and what you value as significant rather than to accept the truth of your present reality? Are you using an **Image** to avoid taking responsibility or, conversely, are you using an **Image** to blame yourself for perceived lack?

■ Shared **Images** often forge groups and alliances; resonant identities share a vision precisely because they have a common experience of the way things are (and should be), utilizing these joint **Images** to unify everyone as they progress toward a mutual goal. Consider the **Image**(s) you share with others as showcased within the **Image** Frame. What does this **Image**(s) communicate about your group and your group's aspirations, in contrast to the way things are now? Do you agree with this **Image**(s)? Why or why not? Does this **Image**(s) distort reality in some way? How does the **Image**(s) benefit or impede what you are trying to achieve? How much denial of reality is revealed upon closer examination of this **Image**(s)?

■ One way of viewing an **Image** is as a blueprint or a mock-up: the map of how we act in the physical universe to work toward the realization of an ideal. What do the contents of the **Image** Frame tell you about your current plans? Have you aligned them with what is actual, or are you allowing your own **Image** of what you wish to get in the way of envisioning and executing the necessary steps to make your goal a reality?

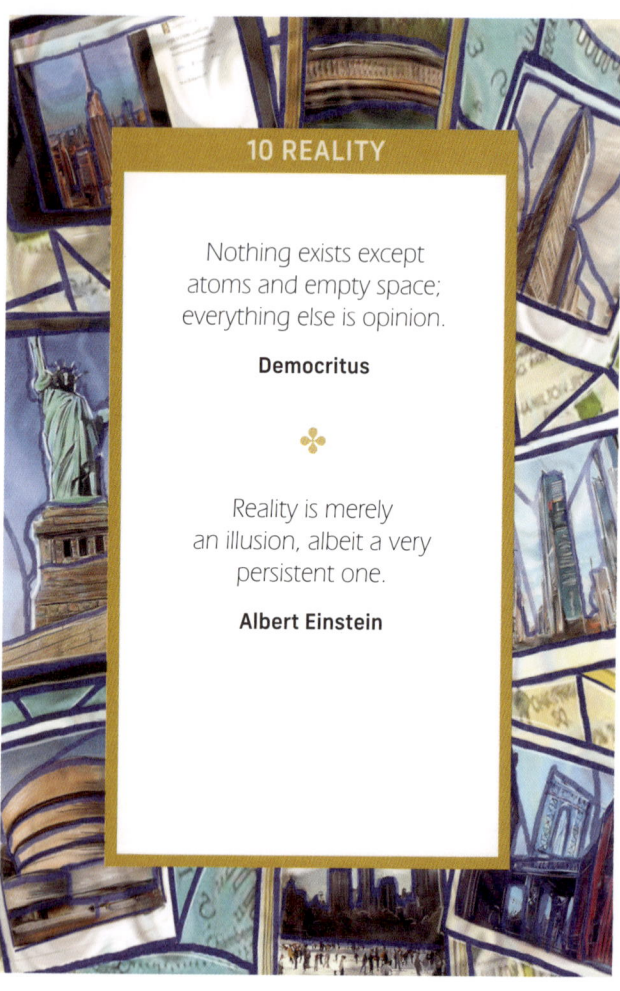

Nothing exists except
atoms and empty space;
everything else is opinion.

Democritus

♣

Reality is merely
an illusion, albeit a very
persistent one.

Albert Einstein

REALITY

Reality is the state of things as they actually exist, as opposed to our images of them. The things in life that are commonly observed and verified to exist by most (if not all), that are consistent as opposed to random or influenced by conformity or mass hysteria. Something that is perceived as "real" and is physically experienced by the senses is generally regarded as **Reality**—but **Reality** is neither truth nor facts.

For we humans, **Reality** is relative, meaning that something real can be considered only in relation to other things deemed real. Some posit that science defines **Reality**, but science measures phenomena, hypothesizes, and makes predictions. At most, science offers workable assumptions (for example, it assumes that whatever **Reality** is, it can be measured), but it does not define **Reality** itself.

Reality is more aptly ascribed to the realm of philosophers, those thinkers throughout history who have questioned the nature of existence itself. In philosophy, *metaphysics* is the study of defining reality and our understanding of it. Once upon a time, **Reality** was determined by what we all could perceive with our physical senses—such as bodies and trees and houses—but as human awareness progressed, our **Reality** expanded far beyond the limited sense organs of the body, to include everything from quasars and galaxies to cells and quarks. Even epistemology, the philosophical study of knowing, still does not promise to establish **Reality**.

How do we define **Reality** apart from our perceptions? Generally, we utilize agreement—whatever most people consider "real"—and those who disagree with the general consensus are judged "delusional" or at the very least "deluded."

If ten people view a traffic accident, they might disagree about who was at fault, the order of the events, and the particulars involved—but usually all ten witnesses will equally attest that a traffic accident occurred. Thus, the accident itself we can assume was a **Reality**—it is only the specifics that are uncertain, muddied by the contradictory perceptions of those who experienced it. Of course, this sort of **Reality** kept the world flat in the minds of humans for much of our history!

Whether we agree that something is real or not—or call it different things, or emphasize diverse aspects, or care about one part more than another—doesn't change its **Reality**. The image we have inside us of **Reality** is a map, but **Reality** itself is the territory (thank you, Korzybski). **Reality** is *what is*, regardless of what we think, agree, feel, imagine, or need it to be.

Ask yourself . . .

■ What do the contents of the **Reality** Frame suggest you are missing, not seeing, or misunderstanding about what you perceive, as opposed to what you think it is, feel it is, imagine it is, agree with others that it must be, or need it to be?

■ **Reality** often asks you to stop and reconsider. Is there some aspect of *what is* that you're deluding yourself about? Gaze into the center of the **Reality** Frame to find what you're omitting or misinterpreting.

■ Sometimes the **Reality** Frame reveals a fundamental unreality not just for yourself, but for a group or even a society of which you're a part. What foundational belief or knowing are you and those around you basing your lives on and enacting in the world as though it were **Reality** that is more mythical than actual? What story are you all re-creating again and again rather than facing (and 'fessing up to) a **Reality** you'd rather not live or admit?

■　**Reality** and facts are not the same thing, although we modern humans often like to pretend it's so, to gain the same surety of action and purpose that religious precepts and commandments gave our ancestors once upon a time. A fact is something that is known to be true—something said to be true or supposed to have happened—but there are many human facts throughout history that have been disproved again and again. The facts of today are often the fodder of tomorrow. What fact do you see within the **Reality** Frame that is far too much belief for you? How are you basing your life on belief in this fact to the detriment of **Reality** and All That Is?

■　One of the beautiful lessons of the **Reality** Frame is to recognize and, it's hoped, appreciate just how remarkable humanity is at creating, inventing, and problem-solving, for it is only out of our honest confrontation of the limitations of **Reality** that we do our most ingenious work. What **Reality** of life displayed in the contents of its Frame are you being challenged to overcome, rise above, or outwit? What **Reality** do you (and possibly humanity) need to acknowledge and, in turn, craft a solution for?

■　**Reality** is composed of both order and chaos, and often our greatest twisting and pretending arises from our desire to create more (or at least the appearance of more) safe order in our lives to avoid the dangerous chaos of **Reality.** As you look within the **Reality** Frame, what of its chaos do you see that you've been afraid to confront? What scares you about accepting **Reality**? How might your life be transformed by releasing this fear? What's in the territory of **Reality** that isn't on your internal map?

■ The **Reality** Frame challenges you to recalibrate your perceptions. Try to see what you've placed within the **Reality** Frame in a new way and from different viewpoints—look at it from as many perspectives as possible. What beliefs, opinions, experiences, and upsets have you placed upon the **Reality** revealed within the Frame's contents that are clouding your vision and making it difficult for you to accurately perceive *what is*?

*Reality
is neither truth
nor facts.*

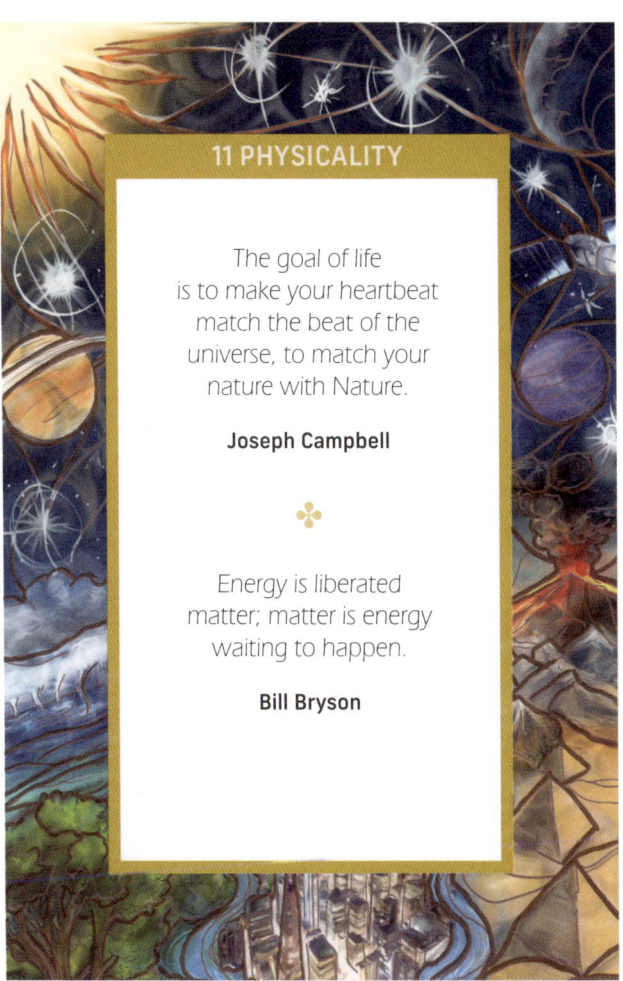

11 PHYSICALITY

The goal of life
is to make your heartbeat
match the beat of the
universe, to match your
nature with Nature.

Joseph Campbell

Energy is liberated
matter; matter is energy
waiting to happen.

Bill Bryson

PHYSICALITY

Physicality encompasses everything that makes up this material universe in which our bodies reside—occupying three-dimensional space that is measurable by height, width, and depth—within the context of the fourth dimension of time. Matter is the basic building block of **Physicality**. It takes up space, has mass, and consists of atoms that are in turn made up of protons, neutrons, and electrons. Quantum physics further suggests that matter is made up of particles or waves (or both), recently positing that fragments of energy are the actual building blocks of **Physicality**.

The Frame of **Physicality** includes yourself, humanity, and all life forms as well as the totality of everything that tangibly exists in our physical environment, the unified whole of the cosmos. From earth to sky to outer (and inner) space, if you can perceive it with the physical senses or scientific instruments, or even demonstrate it with advanced physics, it is a part of **Physicality**.

Ask yourself . . .

■ What vital aspect of **Physicality** is revealed to you through this Frame's contents? Is there an element of **Physicality** with a message for you other than the portions of the physical universe that you regularly interact with? What aspect of **Physicality** speaks to you through this Frame, and what is its vital message for your life today?

■ The **Physicality** Frame might suggest a harmful physical obsession or, conversely, a part of **Physicality** that you are discounting to your own detriment. What part of **Physicality** do you see within the Frame that you're fixated on? What part of **Physicality** do you see that you didn't perceive or recognize before? How does this seem to you?

■   Often, **Physicality** uncovers your impetus or purpose for embodiment into the physical universe. What do you need to know about your sojourn in **Physicality** that might be discovered within this Frame?

■   Do you experience **Physicality** as limitation, as celebration, as mystery, or as something else? Does this viewpoint serve you or hold you back? Look within the **Physicality** Frame for your answer to these questions.

■   The **Physicality** Frame is all about matter—what you might be missing about matter itself, what's the point of the matter, and what matters to you. It also indicates what's really the matter. Find what's your matter displayed (and what might be done about it) within this Frame.

■   The **Physicality** Frame asks you to consider where you're stuck, heavy, serious, fixed, substantial, or dense. What do you need to let go of? How can you release, lighten up, inspire, adjust, be playful, open up?

■   Perhaps what you've placed within the **Physicality** Frame identifies the dimension(s) of existence that is keeping you trapped and transfixed—what makes you small rather than All. Are you content with this truth of your existence, or is it time to choose another way?

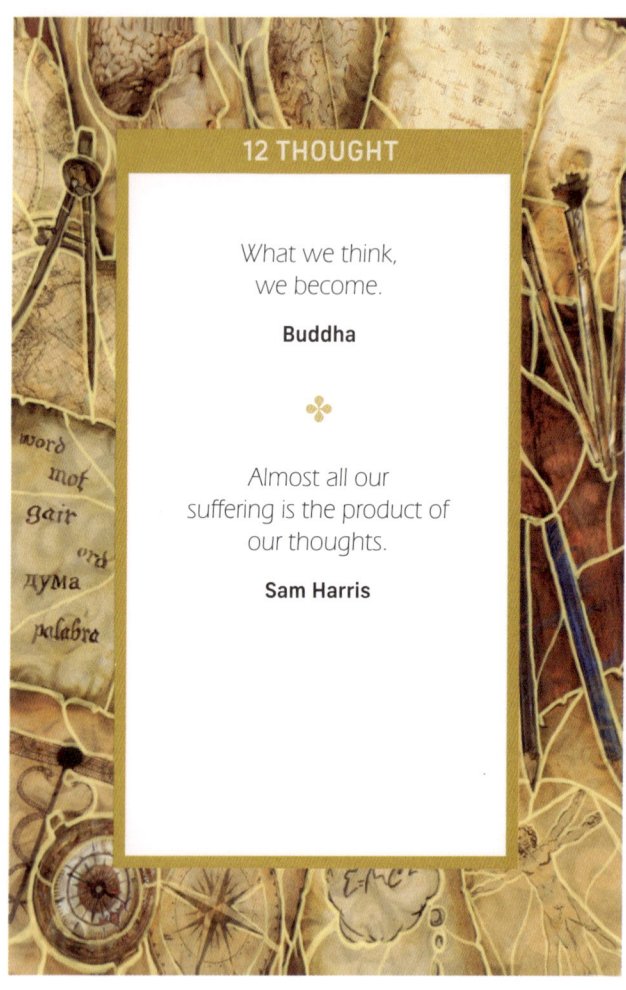

What we think,
we become.

Buddha

Almost all our
suffering is the product of
our thoughts.

Sam Harris

THOUGHT

Thought is the action of thinking, the mental process by which a being forms ideas, opinions, associations, and paradigms. The mind cannot define itself, and thus a dilemma arises in the attempt to define its principal mode of action. Experientially, our **Thought**s seem to occur suddenly in our minds from out of nowhere—they "happen" to us, but then we can either witness their passing like a wave upon the shore or else choose to immerse ourselves in them fully, expanding their reach and effects; when we think this way, we utilize our thoughts to make sense of, interpret, and model the world we experience, making predictions as a result.

Thoughts are initially symbols/ideas/conceptions. As we continue to think, we synthesize (put symbols/ideas/conceptions together) and dissect (take symbols/ideas/conceptions apart). Sometimes, but far from necessarily, **Thought** is the flow of ideas that leads to logical conclusions. Our **Thought**s become the mental representations and cognitive maps that cause us to act in a general direction. Although a **Thought** itself is a short-lived, discrete event, it can become so much more as we manifest our **Thought**s in our lives.

Although this Frame's message can be from or about your own **Thought**s, it might also reveal a communication from another's **Thought**s or even from the realm of **Thought** itself. **Ask yourself . . .**

■ **Thought** wishes to give you a vital message about what you've placed within its Frame: Will you receive it, acknowledge it, and let it continue on to its next recipient, or is **Thought**'s message one you need to grapple with and use to reshape and influence your own paradigms and conclusions?

■   Now is the time to examine your own **Thought**s. What **Thought** is shown within the Frame that you might need to consider further (or reconsider)? What alluded **Thought** might you be avoiding? What divulged **Thought** is serving you? What exposed **Thought** is holding you back?

■   Often, **Thought** addresses us when we are fixated on our emotions to the detriment of rationality. Are your moods overwhelming your lucidity right now? Examine your own **Thought**s and reasoning as revealed within this Frame—maybe a refresher in logical fallacies and formal logic is due? Conversely, does this encourage your current thinking?

■   What **Thought** from another (or others) do you need to consider that is unveiled in the **Thought** Frame? On the other hand, you might see a **Thought** from another (or others) that is influencing you and needs to be rejected.

■   Are you thinking any **Thought**s that are not your own? What is their actual source? Are these **Thought**s helping or harming you?

■   **Thought** asks you to understand the difference between thinking your **Thought**s, feeling your **Thought**s, having your **Thought**s, and believing your **Thought**s. Just because you have a **Thought** doesn't make it so (or not so). Examine the **Thought** suggested by what you've placed inside the Frame, distance yourself from it, and determine if it is true or false.

■   Within this Frame see your relationship with **Thought**. Where do **Thought**s come from? Do you believe you *are* your **Thought**s, or do your **Thought**s seem like unwanted intruders?

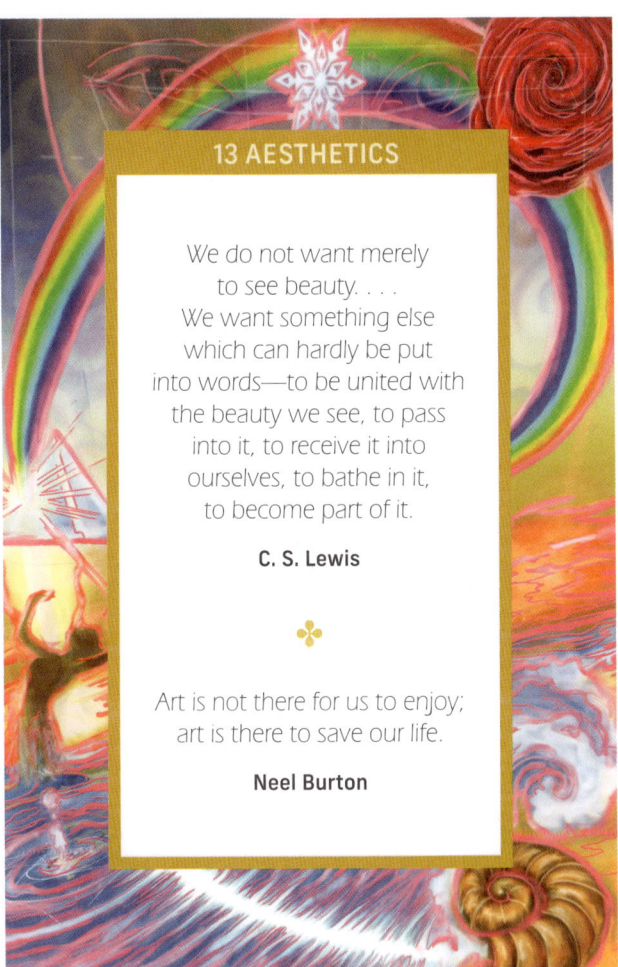

13 AESTHETICS

We do not want merely
to see beauty. . . .
We want something else
which can hardly be put
into words—to be united with
the beauty we see, to pass
into it, to receive it into
ourselves, to bathe in it,
to become part of it.

C. S. Lewis

❧

Art is not there for us to enjoy;
art is there to save our life.

Neel Burton

AESTHETICS

The word **Aesthetics** comes from the Greek word for perception, *aesthesis*. **Aesthetics** is the Frame that governs the nature and appreciation of beauty—what we deem pleasurable to perceive—especially with regard to art and its visceral ability to evoke an emotive response within us. The **Aesthetics** Frame conveys the patterns of interrelations reflecting order that are pleasing to behold, and the expression of serenity of beingness throughout the physical universe. Think of **Aesthetics** as our clue to the Source and universal order of All.

While some insist that "beauty is in the eye of the beholder," the study of **Aesthetics** proposes an underlying symmetry in the things we find beautiful—from the golden ratio / golden mean / divine proportion of mathematics to the holographic principle of physics, that the seed of All is within every piece. Beauty makes us cry because in it we glimpse for a moment the full expression of self as All and then feel the intense agony of loss as we both remember and experience anew the shattering of this wholeness into pieces. This underlying **Aesthetic** order reveals the beautiful oneness we have lost in the fall or shattering: **Aesthetics** is the Tao, losing oneself in the action itself, and all things engaged as a single expression of All.

Aesthetics is found in those mountaintop moments of perfect serendipity, synchronicity, and epiphany that reveal but a glimpse of the hidden hints of the order of creation itself, the hand of creator in the created. When under the sway of the **Aesthetics** Frame, we revere and appreciate the thing for what it is in itself and as a reflection of the All rather than for what it does for us.

Ask yourself . . .

◼ Gaze into what you have placed within the **Aesthetics** Frame. Do you find it beautiful? Why or why not? What feelings does it awaken within you? How do you see yourself (or not-self) reflected? How do you see All reflected? Do you perceive the All in yourself? Can you perceive yourself reflected in All?

◼ What do you need to see, acknowledge, or release about your perceptions/opinions/beliefs about beauty (or the lack thereof) as revealed within what you see in the **Aesthetics** Frame?

◼ Look into the **Aesthetics** Frame and ask yourself: What do you see that gives you pleasure in the physical world? What do you see that you find unpleasurable? What does this say about you and your embodiment?

◼ Is there an aspect of **Aesthetics** inside the Frame that you have been ignoring? Is there an aspect of **Aesthetics** that troubles you? Is there an aspect of **Aesthetics** that consumes you?

◼ **Aesthetics** calls to you to examine your art—both what you admire and long for as well as what you create. How important is art in your life? How does art make you uncomfortable? What art do you dislike, and what does this reveal about you? Is it time to expand or alter the artistry of your life? Consider the contents of the **Aesthetics** Frame for further insight into these questions.

■ Do you feel attraction or repulsion in response to what you see within the **Aesthetics** Frame? What do you find beautiful? What do you find ugly? What does this say about your relationship with yourself and reality? Are you content with the beauty in your life? Can you engage differently with the world to make your life more beautiful?

■ Often, the images we see within the **Aesthetics** Frame depict our relationship with beauty (or lack thereof). Do you trust and value your own perceptions of beauty? Do you judge yourself or others on the basis of whether or not you find them beautiful or pleasurable? Are you using **Aesthetics** to find yourself or others lacking?

Think of Aesthetics as our clue to the Source and universal order of All.

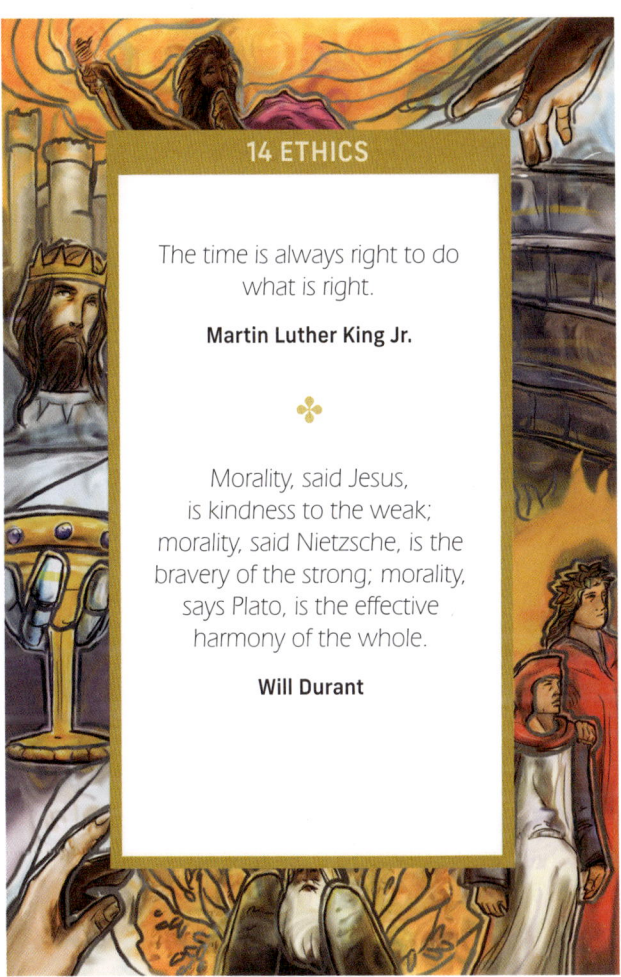

14 ETHICS

The time is always right to do
what is right.

Martin Luther King Jr.

❖

Morality, said Jesus,
is kindness to the weak;
morality, said Nietzsche, is the
bravery of the strong; morality,
says Plato, is the effective
harmony of the whole.

Will Durant

ETHICS

Philosophically, **Ethics** is defined as the study of the code of right/wrong and good/bad as enacted by a person or group. The **Ethics** Frame indicates embodiment of awareness of truth in accordance with external order and one's personal responsibility, regardless of how a person or situation changes.

Practically, **Ethics** is an internal code of conduct and responsibility, policed by self rather than others (thus *response-ability*, or our ability to respond appropriately to what is).

Spiritually, **Ethics** Frames a central flaw in the human capacity for goodness. When one of us harms another, it is necessary to see the other as not-self (or separate). Harmful/bad/evil action is predicated on this lie of separateness. Even self-harm finds its roots in the lie of self-separation. No harm can be justified, though many have justifications as a substitute for responsibility. In truth, there are only choices and consequences. Justifying our bad or evil acts both conceals our responsibility and springs from the lie of not-me. Consequent to this false separateness, we convince ourselves that we are not responsible for the other.

Our sense of **Ethics** is the pervading awareness of the original postulate (I am) that's underneath the altered postulate (I am not), and thus ethical action is acting in truth to honor and taking responsibility for the other (and even all) as oneself.

Ask yourself . . .

■ What is **Ethics** communicating to me today through or about the contents of its Frame? What am I ignoring about **Ethics**? What am I over-preoccupied with concerning **Ethics**?

■ Often, the **Ethics** Frame calls you to reach beyond yourself, your own concerns, and what you want or need to take up your responsibility to the external order and those around you. What responsibilities do you see within the **Ethics** Frame today? Are you living up to your responsibilities? Are you responding appropriately to what is?

■ Perhaps what you see within the **Ethics** Frame challenges your actions and assumptions. Are you harming another or others? Using justification not to take responsibility for your action or inaction? The **Ethics** Frame can warn us to watch out for unethical behavior—our own, another's, or others'.

■ Does something you see in the contents of the **Ethics** Frame urge you to accept responsibility for something or someone? On the other hand, might what's within the **Ethics** Frame indicate that you're taking responsibility for something or someone that is not yours to take?

■ Consider what's inside the **Ethics** Frame about those whom you deem wrong, bad, or evil. Often, those we judge or find fault with reveal much more about ourselves than the people we criticize. How is seeing the other as not-self, rather than oneself, justifying your willingness to condemn or wish harm?

■ Does the message of what you've placed within the **Ethics** Frame seem confused, muddled, or ambiguous to you? When this happens, it might be a subtle signal to study **Ethics** and reexamine your own ethical/moral code or the ethical code you follow because of the groups, society, or culture of which you are a part. Take a photo of the **Ethics** Frame and what you've placed within it to use as you seek to understand this message more clearly during your studies and self-reflection, trusting that with honest inquiry, all will become clear.

■ Do you follow your own code of **Ethics**? Are you breaking your code of **Ethics**? Do you use your own code of **Ethics** to violate the ethical code of another? Within the **Ethics** Frame, find your answer to these vital paths of inquiry.

In truth, there are only choices and consequences. Justifying our bad or evil acts both conceals our responsibility and springs from the lie of not-me.

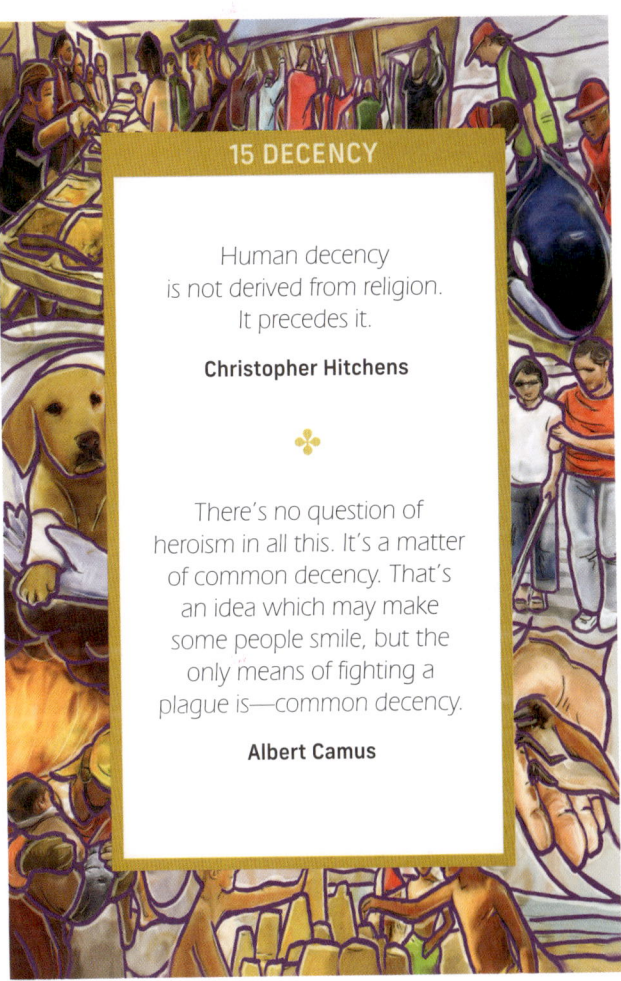

15 DECENCY

Human decency
is not derived from religion.
It precedes it.

Christopher Hitchens

❖

There's no question of
heroism in all this. It's a matter
of common decency. That's
an idea which may make
some people smile, but the
only means of fighting a
plague is—common decency.

Albert Camus

DECENCY

Decency can seem a vague notion in a modern world where all is relatively reduced to winning, being right, and feeling good. The **Decency** Frame beckons us to virtue. **Decency** is doing what is best and right within circumstances that would have been easier had we just joined the prevailing opinion.

Decency is the code of conduct unquestioned by all innately—it's so ubiquitous, we often call it "common decency," and it's so ingrained into existence that no one (who is honest) questions it, since from a spiritual perspective it predates biological life. For example, we might argue that it is wrong to murder (morality), or we might argue the responsible taking of human life (ethics), but no decent person would argue in favor of raping and killing a newborn baby.

One way to understand **Decency** is this: Good people do moral things and great people do ethical things, but **Decency** arises from what unites us all, from being the Source of All in One. It's as though a divine hand reaches through us to improve existence for each and all. **Decency** is neither having goodness nor acting ethically, but an extension of Being the Order that pervades Everything. Sometimes **Decency** boggles our human rationality, yet we viscerally "just know" when someone acts decently.

Ask yourself . . .

■ The **Decency** Frame demands you to consider what its contents suggest to be the best (if most difficult) action for all involved in this situation. How is **Decency** lacking right now?

What is holding back those involved from doing the decent thing? Face this barrier and choose decent action.

■ Who or what is communicating with you about **Decency** today through this Frame? Does it surprise you? Does it scare you? What right action is All asking of you today?

■ Is there a decent act you are avoiding? Are you repressing or denying **Decency**? Might you be rationalizing an indecent act? What aspect of **Decency** are you opposing? If you feel defeated right now, is it because you are denying the decent course of action? **Decency** appeals to you to get off the sidelines and do the decent thing—will you answer the call? Look to the Frame's contents to identify the decent action.

■ Often, acts of **Decency** can bring the decent individual pain and suffering as a result of challenging the status quo in a selfish and corrupt world. Are you confused by your suffering for doing the decent thing? The **Decency** Frame indicates your path to peace.

■ What you see within the **Decency** Frame might challenge your stable data, beliefs, and opinions about who is wrong, bad, or undeserving in your life, and ask you to get past your upset, your resentment, and your rightness to reach to the heart of what connects us all. Can you rise above those you fear or despise to act in such a way as to improve the trajectory of All That Is rather than simply furthering your own interests, judgments, and beliefs?

■   You might believe that you are acting morally or ethically, but when you gaze into the **Decency** Frame, is there a quiet voice deep inside you whispering what you know to be the decent thing? Will you listen or will you continue to allow self-interest, group pressure, and societal myths to determine your present ignoble course of action?

■   What does common decency dictate in this situation? Just do it. **Decency** begs you to cease hesitating as a result of how you will be perceived or what others will think, or because of possible repercussions to yourself; it's time to do what you know deep within to be the right action. Let what you've placed within the **Decency** Frame be your guide.

Decency is doing what is best and right within circumstances that would have been easier had we just joined the prevailing opinion.

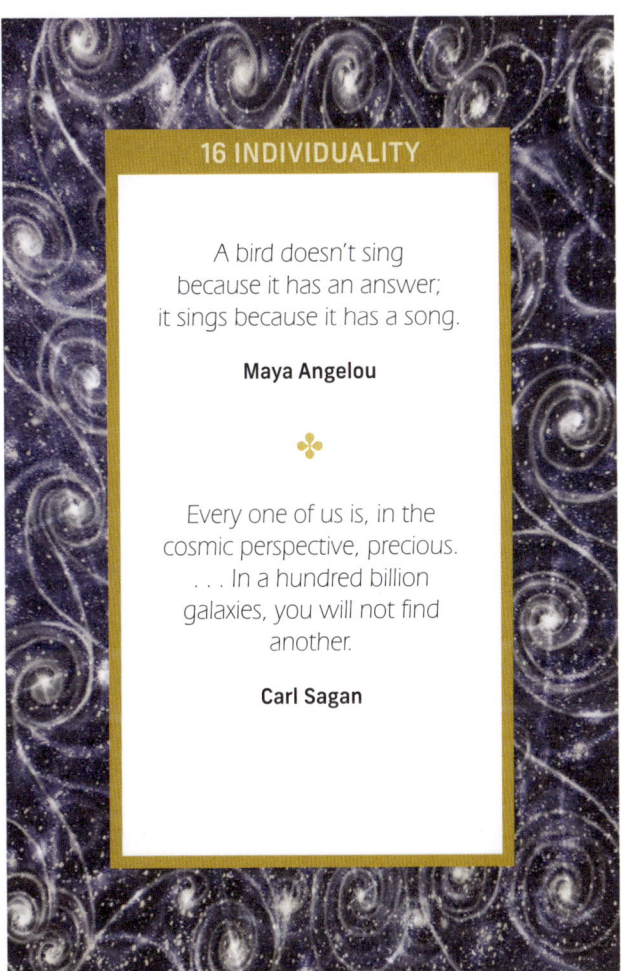

16 INDIVIDUALITY

A bird doesn't sing
because it has an answer;
it sings because it has a song.

Maya Angelou

Every one of us is, in the
cosmic perspective, precious.
. . . In a hundred billion
galaxies, you will not find
another.

Carl Sagan

INDIVIDUALITY

One odd (but isn't everything about **Individuality** by definition odd?) synonym for **Individuality** is *singularity*, archaically that which is singular (separate, unusual, and distinctive), and scientifically a point in space where there is a mass with infinite density (infinities, by the way, cannot be contained by mere physicality or mind).

Individuals have selves, but only for a time. Your **Individuality** is your sovereign I Am, what you initially decided you are not, the lie that you are not All—it is the eternal individuation, beyond time and space, and that which continues after this lifetime.

Individuality is the infinitely small point or static within each of us that cannot be divided, the watcher that watches the watcher. What one is being can be divided into pieces, what one is doing can be stopped, and what one is having can be lost or fractured, but the I am that I am, the actual individual beingness, is indivisible and unique.

Ask yourself . . .

■ What message is **Individuality** communicating through what it Frames today about you as an individual being?

■ **Individuality** asks you to compare and contrast your **Individuality** and your identity (consider using Frame One: Identity for further exploration). What is your **Individuality** from an eternal perspective as opposed to your current identity's temporal perspective?

■ How is who you really are different from what you are being, what you are doing, and what you have? What preoccupies, deceives, and pacifies you? The **Individuality** Frame beseeches you to ask and answer the larger questions of existence now, before you have to start the process of embodiment all over again.

■ Often, what most transfixes us in a lifetime are the topics, issues, and situations that bother both our **Individuality** and our identity, for these similarities create a resonance that disrupts the **Individual**'s ability to offer clarity to oneself. Do the contents of the **Individuality** Frame echo one of these joint difficulties? Is it time to release this stuck attention?

■ Choosing this Frame always suggests the need to separate from the world for a time and voyage within—through isolation, meditation, stillness, contemplation, and **Individual** reflection. How can you set aside the time you need to create this essential sacred space?

■ The **Individuality** Frame asks you who you truly are at your very core. Can you reach the watcher within you? How are you singular . . . separate . . . unusual . . . distinctive . . . unique? What do you see in the contents of the **Individuality** Frame that existed before your birth and will continue past the death of all your identities?

■ Ultimately, **Individuality** calls you to remember the initial incident wherein you decided you are not, the initial lie that you are somehow not All. How is this reflected in what you've Framed?

17 GUARDIANS

Maybe when we face a tragedy, someone, somewhere is preventing a bigger tragedy from happening.

Kamand Kojouri

❧

No, I never saw an angel, but it is irrelevant whether I saw one or not. I feel their presence around me.

Paulo Coelho

GUARDIANS

Guardians are our protectors and guides. They have been called angel, ascended master, spirit guide, animal ally, ancestor, higher self, and many other titles throughout the ages. **Guardians** may appear to us incarnated or incorporeal, but what all **Guardians** have in common is that they have agreed to watch over us, intercede on our behalf, inspire as well as encourage us, and deliver messages—but not interfere with our freedom to choose. **Guardians** may be invisible to us, some we can see clearly, while still others we perceive but cannot see.

Guardians respond to us when we ask or call them, and are motivated by altruistic intentions for the benefit of one within the order of All.

Guardians are not as we are—although they might *seem* to manifest themselves to us via a relatable image, name, or character, they are more wave to our particle. Some serve as personal guides, but many **Guardians** are quite impersonal, solely concerning themselves with principalities, significant events, and averting large-scale chaos. Envision existence as a river flowing in a particular direction that is the sum total of all the beings involved and their intentions merging, retreating, and interacting within its banks. **Guardians** are the currents and eddies that carry us in a specific direction, whether hastening our progression or shifting a course correction. **Guardians** freely offer their abundant channels of energy to empower us, providing us the wavelengths, resonance, and emanations necessary to alter our own direction.

Ask yourself . . .

■ Your **Guardians** have a message for you—its meaning can be found within the **Guardians** Frame. What are the **Guardians** counseling you today?

■ Is there a specific **Guardian** reaching out to you? Look to the contents of the **Guardians** Frame to find out who is speaking, and receive the message. Is it possible that someone else's **Guardians** are using this Frame to communicate their intentions to you today?

■ Are you being called to act as a **Guardian** in someone else's life? Gaze into the contents of the **Guardians** Frame to understand whom you need to guide and how to proceed.

■ Have you been blind to or ignoring your **Guardians'** influence in your life? Is it time to open yourself to their message and guidance? It's time to pay attention. Heed your **Guardians'** wise guidance revealed through the contents of the **Guardians** Frame.

■ Sometimes your **Guardians** may be cautioning that you have been following flawed advice and allowing yourself to be fooled by harmful influences, whether human or supernatural. Pay close attention to the contents of the **Guardians** Frame as to its source and substance. However, always remember that in the end, you are responsible for yourself and your outcomes. You must choose whether or not to follow your **Guardians'** guidance—it is perfectly acceptable to choose a different way, because the consequences are yours and yours alone.

■ Your **Guardians** ask you to look beyond your concerns of this moment and consider the long-term outcomes of your choices for yourself, both in this lifetime and within the context of eternity. What habits, choices, and beliefs does this Frame reveal you are enacting that are breeding lasting consequences for you, those around you, and those still to be?

■ Is the **Guardians** Frame asking you to release your current agreements with your **Guardians** and either find your own way for a time or else seek new **Guardians** for guidance? Consider the contents of the **Guardians** Frame to direct this change in your life.

Guardians are the currents and eddies that carry us in a specific direction, whether hastening our progression or shifting a course correction.

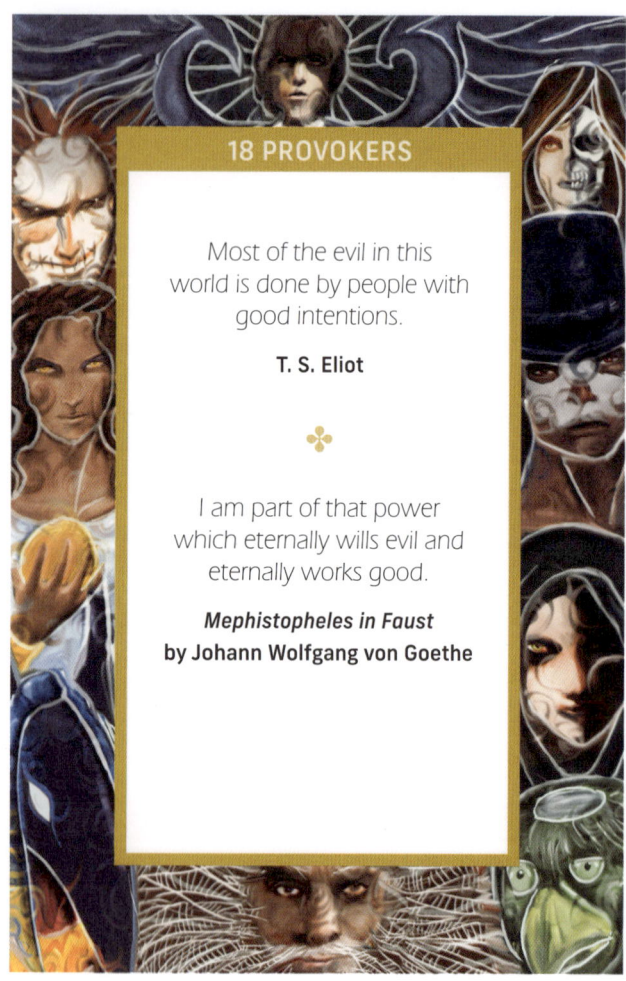

Most of the evil in this world is done by people with good intentions.

T. S. Eliot

❖

I am part of that power which eternally wills evil and eternally works good.

Mephistopheles in Faust
by Johann Wolfgang von Goethe

PROVOKERS

Provokers are those who challenge us, bother us, tempt us, stop us, harm us, oppose us, and destroy us. They are our villains and antagonists, our hated and despised. Without **Provokers**, our lives would be peaceful and exactly what we think we wish/want/deserve—and thus they seem to be the source of our problems, pain, and suffering. They are our scapegoats and simultaneously what provoke us to progress and overcome.

A **Provoker** is the catalyst that triggers a reaction to transform our inertia, apathy, and inaction.

Provokers may be physical, supernatural, spiritual, or aspects of self that harm or hinder us. Devils, demons, and fallen angels. Trickster gods. Malevolent spirits described by any culture or tradition. Enemies. Adversaries. Frailties, defects, and tragic flaws. Any being or aspect of ourselves or existence that stands in our way might communicate through the **Provokers** Frame.

Ask yourself . . .

■ A **Provoker** has a disturbing message for you, communicated via the contents of this Frame—one you probably don't want to accept but need to heed. Will you listen?

■ Are you placing yourself in the dangerous path of **Provokers**? Be wary of poking these sleeping tigers—for **Provokers** will most definitely bite if you attract their interest, wreaking havoc in your life. Perhaps you secretly wish to bring down the wrath of the **Provokers** upon yourself for some reason? What do you see within the **Provokers** Frame about these problematic choices?

■ Does what you glimpse within the **Provokers** Frame suggest that you yourself have become a **Provoker**? Are you opposing or getting in someone else's way? Is your provocation misguided or self-serving? Conversely, are you precisely the **Provoker** that the other needs? Is there a message for you to give another as **Provoker**?

■ Might what you see revealed within the **Provoker** Frame warn that you have become your own worst **Provoker**? Why are you doing this to yourself? Is it time to quit self-sabotaging behaviors and seek outside or professional help? On the other hand, you might be insulating yourself too much and need to be provoked! Consider the contents of the **Provokers** Frame for direction in these matters.

■ Often, this Frame cautions one to be wary of complacency, pretense, and ingratitude. What do the contents of the **Provokers** Frame expose about your denial of responsibility? The longer you evade taking responsibility for your errors, omissions, and misdeeds—the longer you persist in refusing to acknowledge the truth and act to improve yourself and your situation—the more **Provokers** will find you and stir up trouble in your life.

■ Is there a **Provoker** in your life whose influence you need to escape? Look to the contents of the **Provokers** Frame for clues as to how to reject this **Provoker's** hold on you.

■ Are you playing the blame game, accusing others of being **Provokers** when you should thank them or realize it's your own damn fault for granting them power? Gaze into this Frame to see if you're unduly accusing others of being **Provokers**.

The world is full of magic things, patiently waiting for our senses to grow sharper.

William Butler Yeats

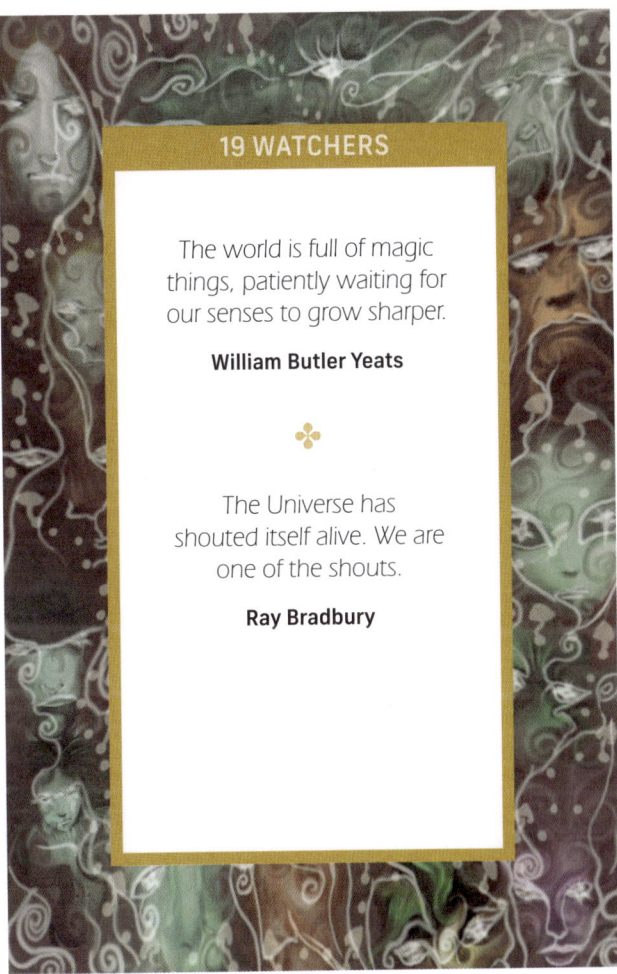

The Universe has shouted itself alive. We are one of the shouts.

Ray Bradbury

WATCHERS

Awareness of the **Watchers**, when we allow ourselves to perceive them at all, makes most humans vaguely uncomfortable. Of course, our mythologies and legends and stories are full of their strange otherness, but by and large, most believe them to be humanity's own fantastical imaginings (or delusions).

The **Watchers** for the most part don't get involved or care much at all about humanity's machinations and dramas, except as they occasionally affect the **Watchers** themselves. **Watchers** can be found everywhere—inside and outside, adjacent and distant, below and above—in this world and dimension as well as throughout other dimensions and worlds. The **Watchers** Frame includes extraterrestrials and ultraterrestrials, Sidhe and faerie folk, goblins and dragons, ghosts and other shadowy entities whom most have sometimes glimpsed and later come to either sense or fear.

Ask yourself . . .

■ Are **Watchers** speaking to you right now through this Frame and what it encloses? Is a **Watcher** using the contents of the Frame to communicate with you? Is what you've placed within the Frame a **Watcher** that you've never acknowledged before? Listen to the message and consider its portent for you, your life, and possibly humanity as a whole.

■ Have you been disregarding or ignoring **Watchers**? If so, why? Is it fear of the **Watchers** themselves? Are you worried about seeming foolish, irrational, insane, or weird? Do your beliefs contradict the possibility of their existence? Do you mistrust your own perceptions? Why do you believe that your impressions must be like those around you? Conversely, do you desperately want to believe in the **Watchers** so much that you doubt yourself? Is this blindness serving you or hindering your development? Gaze into the contents of the **Watchers** Frame to comprehend the true reason for your denial.

■ What does this Frame and its contents reveal to you about the nature of **Watchers**? How are they like you? How are they different? Are they safe? How do their interests differ from our own? What can we learn from them? What could they learn from us? Look inside the **Watchers** Frame to see how your path crosses theirs at the crossroads today.

■ Is there a **Watcher** (or **Watchers**) whom you need to protect yourself from? Perhaps you've captured a **Watcher's** notice that is mischievous or harmful to you in some way? Look to what you've placed within the **Watchers** Frame to see your way to safety.

■ Sometimes the **Watchers** Frame nudges you to consider embracing your own otherness—your strangeness, your eccentricity, your oddity, and your nonhuman qualities. Is there some aspect of yourself or a kinship you share with the **Watchers** that you've been blocking? Look to what the **Watchers** Frame surrounds to discover this hidden connection.

■ Is it time to make contact with the **Watchers**? Do you need to research, meditate, astrally project, travel to a specific location, or simply take a walk in nature to discover them? Explore what you've placed inside the **Watchers** Frame to find them.

■ Is a **Watcher** watching something that you also need to notice? Do you need to play the role of a **Watcher** yourself right now? Gaze into the **Watcher** Frame to find your answers.

The Watchers Frame includes extraterrestrials and ultraterrestrials, Sidhe and faerie folk, goblins and dragons, ghosts and other shadowy entities whom most have sometimes glimpsed and later come to either sense or fear.

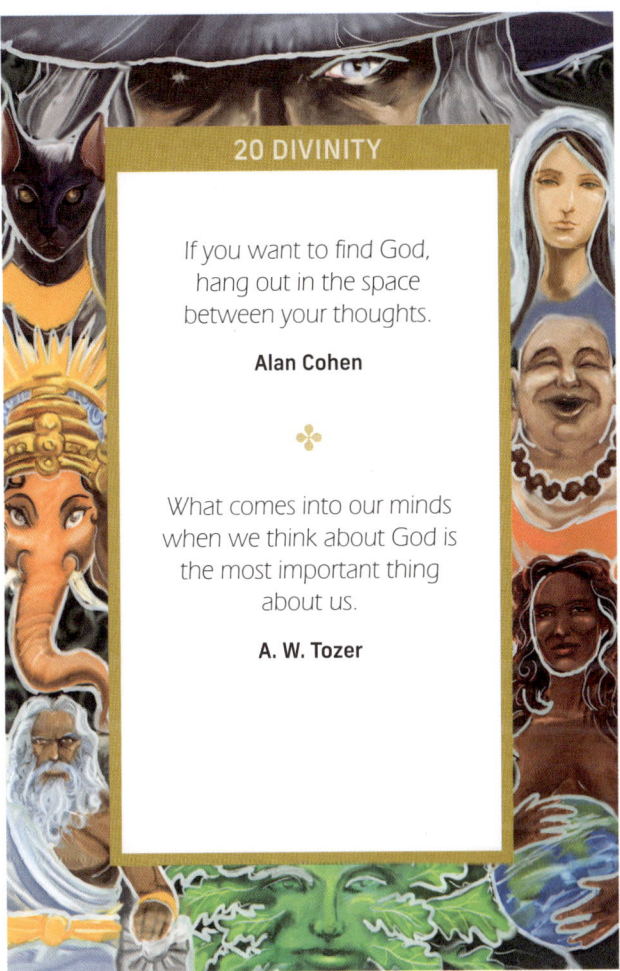

If you want to find God,
hang out in the space
between your thoughts.

Alan Cohen

❖

What comes into our minds
when we think about God is
the most important thing
about us.

A. W. Tozer

DIVINITY

Divinity means "being of, from, or like a God or god."

Divinity encompasses all deities from every religion or spirituality, whether traditional or alternative—monotheistic, polytheistic, or pantheistic. This Frame channels messages from a Larger Being beyond oneself who is able to exert greater control over the physical universe and produce desired results that to humanity seem magical, ineffable, or transcendent. Any being higher or more powerful than oneself might communicate via the **Divinity** Frame.

If gods and goddesses are not speaking to you, the **Divinity** Frame is also static, the nothing that we the incarnated wish we could have. All That Is as One Entity. The All in the One, reflected in every piece. That which unifies all of us to shatter us again and again. **Divinity** is the Source. Where we come from and where we shall return to. The Spark of the Creative Urge that ignites each and All.

Ask yourself . . .

■ Is there a specific **Divinity** or group of divinities speaking to you right now through this Frame and its contents? Is **Divinity** revealing itself to you?

■ What do you see revealed within this Frame about the nature of **Divinity**? What is your relationship with **Divinity**? How is **Divinity** harmful? How is **Divinity** helpful? Is there something in your relationship with **Divinity** that you need to consider, change, enrich, intensify, or discard?

■ Is there an aspect of **Divinity** or a specific **Divinity** that you have been avoiding or blind to? Examine this not-knowing and decide whether or not it serves you. Sometimes this Frame can indicate a problematic divine influence that one has been ignoring—what do the contents of this Frame tell you about your not-seeing? Should you strengthen your boundaries or change course and open up to this divine pressure?

■ Is there a new **Divinity** reaching out to you through this Frame? Is there a **Divinity** that you've accepted who is hindering or hurting you? Is there a larger/higher **Divinity** that you should be concerned with? Is it time to change allegiances or beliefs? Look inside the **Divinity** Frame for direction.

■ Often this Frame suggests it is time to reconsider your place within the broader context of All That Is. Who, what, and where are you within the course of **Divinity**, history, reality, and existence? Where do you wish to be? What is your current trajectory? Does what you've placed within the **Divinity** Frame advise that it's time to make a course correction?

■ Consider the **Divinity** Frame's message as arising from source rather than a specific divine being, providence, intervention, or manifestation. What does the **Divinity** Frame's contents signify as the source or origination of who you are today—your thoughts, your ideas, your beliefs, your direction? Are you your own source, or is another person, group, belief system, deity, etc. your source? What **Divinity** is acting through you?

■ Examine the beliefs about **Divinity** shown in this Frame. Do you suspect you are divine, know someone who is divine, receive divine messages, or have no discourse with **Divinity**? Is there a belief you need to let go of or else embrace?

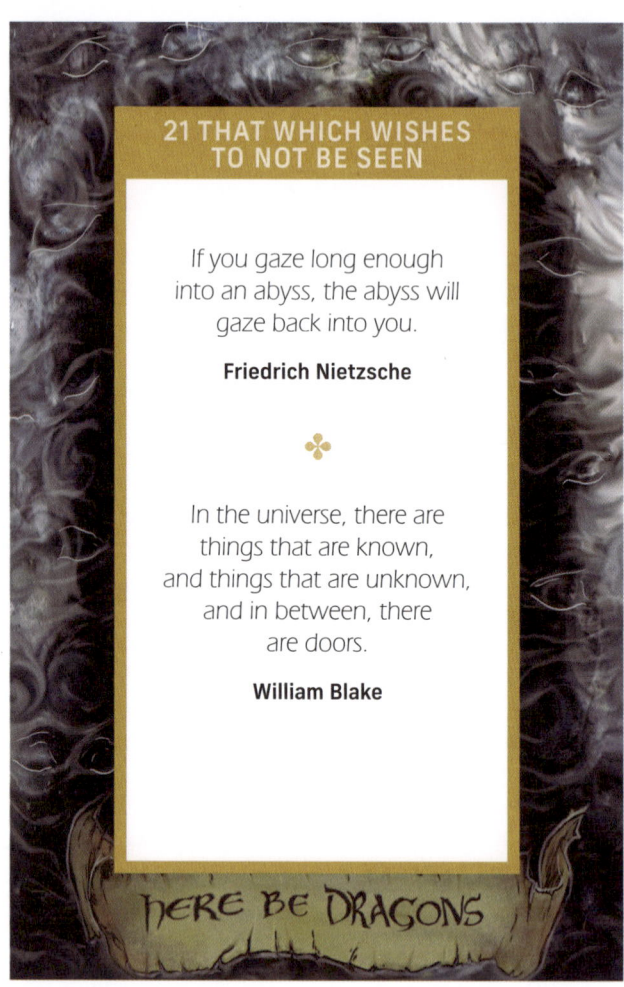

21 THAT WHICH WISHES TO NOT BE SEEN

If you gaze long enough into an abyss, the abyss will gaze back into you.

Friedrich Nietzsche

♣

In the universe, there are things that are known, and things that are unknown, and in between, there are doors.

William Blake

HERE BE DRAGONS

THAT WHICH WISHES TO NOT BE SEEN

Have you ever unequivocally known something but cannot explain how? Had a sneaking but persistent premonition, a sixth sense, a gut feeling, or even heard a quietly whispered message in the dark of the night that you cannot substantiate? **That Which Wishes to Not Be Seen** is speaking to (or through) you. Just as mapmakers of old wrote, "Here be dragons" to denote unexplored or unknown regions, we often imagine **That Which Wishes to Not Be Seen** as monstrous and refuse to acknowledge even the possibility they might exist.

There are beings who do not wish to be seen but nevertheless have something to say. Perhaps they remain in shadows because they appear as monsters to us. Maybe they do not . . . entirely . . . trust us. Mayhap they hide their faces because if we recognized them through the lens of our own biases and limited perspectives, we would not listen. Sometimes it is that they are unwilling to alter themselves in the ways necessary for us to perceive them. There's a chance that someone you think you know very well (but who is hiding pieces of themselves and their truths from you) will voice their secrets via this Frame. If there is a part of yourself you are denying or cannot see, it uses this Frame to communicate with you. Channel the great mysteries with this Frame. Within the bottomless contents of **That Which Wishes to Not Be Seen**, gaze deeply into the abyss few mortals dare to cross, to perchance obtain the holy grail and bring it back to save this ailing realm.

But beware. Be respectful. Be true. **That Which Wishes to Not Be Seen** has its reasons for reaching for us, and these reasons are not our own. In the abyss we humans find the treasures and enlightenment we so desperately seek, but it also drives others of us stark raving mad.

Ask yourself . . .

■ **That Which Wishes to Not Be Seen** has a message for you—what is the message revealed within the contents of this Frame? Why might the speaker be hiding from you?

■ Often the **That Which Wishes to Not Be Seen** Frame prods you to ask yourself to examine those parts of yourself you are blocking, or of which you've chosen to be unconscious. What do you see within the Frame that exposes places of unconsciousness or your own subconscious (or both)? Are there any feelings, thoughts, urges, or memories you've repressed? What are these shadow pieces telling you today?

■ **That Which Wishes to Not Be Seen** can caution of hidden dangers that must be seen and acknowledged to endure them. What is within the **That Which Wishes to Not Be Seen** Frame that points you toward a hazard of which you've been oblivious?

■ Sometimes the most important communication from **That Which Wishes to Not Be Seen** is that you need to stop depending on your physical senses for a time. Once you've seen all there is to see in the contents of this Frame—close your eyes, quiet your mind, still yourself, focus on what you recall, and journey first within and then beyond and into the mysteries to uncover the message of this Frame for you today.

■ **That Which Wishes to Not Be Seen** might divulge entities that have attached themselves to you like discarnate parasites—beings that you at one point consciously or unconsciously entered into an agreement with that keeps you bound together. What do the contents of the **That Which Wishes to Not Be Seen** Frame reveal about the nature of this entity? What resonance merges you together? How does this connection serve you or the entity? Do you wish to continue this relationship or sever your ties, bidding goodbye to **That Which Wishes to Not Be Seen**?

■ Do the contents of the **That Which Wishes to Not Be Seen** Frame allude to something obscured in shadow that needs to come to light? Is there something hidden about a relationship, an alliance, an authority, or another communication source?

■ Are you focused on discovering the secrets of **That Which Wishes to Not Be Seen** in order to avoid your present reality in some way? If not, do you distrust **That Which Wishes to Not Be Seen** purely because you cannot "see" them? Are you captivated with mysteries of any sort, either out of curiosity or suspicion? If you're willing to, gaze into the **That Which Wishes to Not Be Seen** Frame to find out what the unseen think of your attention, and perhaps alter your own trajectory as a result.

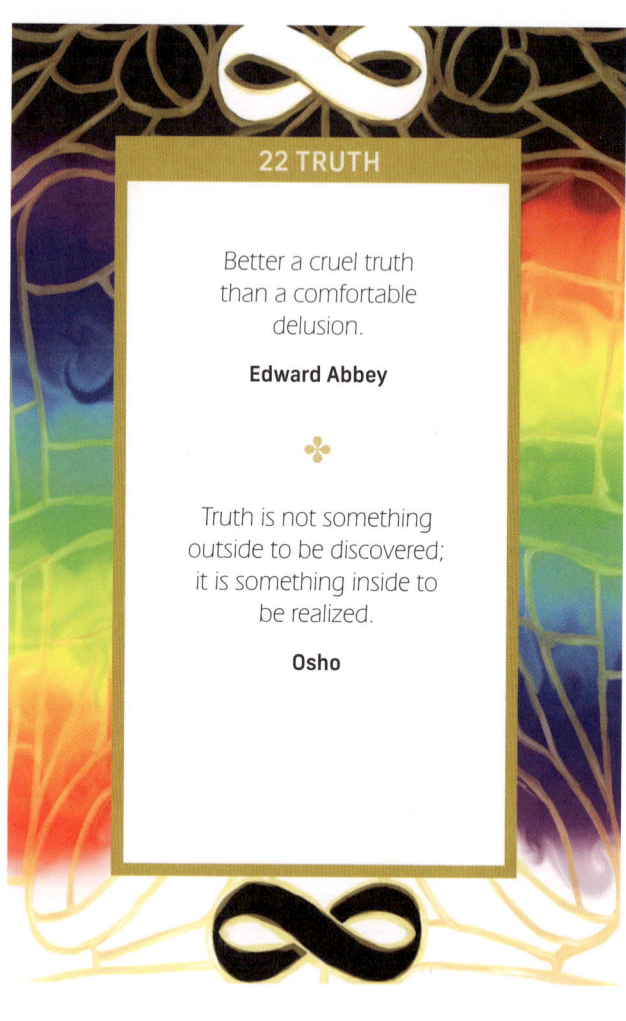

22 TRUTH

Better a cruel truth
than a comfortable
delusion.

Edward Abbey

❖

Truth is not something
outside to be discovered;
it is something inside to
be realized.

Osho

TRUTH

Truth is not what you want it to be; it simply is. Its discovery inspires a certainty and knowing without reservation. **Truth** does not need us to defend it, for it is what it is regardless of human purposes, emotions, viewpoints, beliefs, or ideals. Honesty is not **Truth** (although it is a good place to start), for people can say what they think or feel to be so to the best of their ability yet still not tell the **Truth**.

Some spend entire lifetimes looking for the **Truth** by learning and aligning with others, believing that only what lasts or endures is true. Others determine that there is but One **Truth** that underlies everything, unifying existence, and they pursue finding this commonality as though it's a mysterious key unlocking the answer to all problems. Our first mistake is using our minds to uncover **Truth**, for although minds are useful tools for organization, reason, and judgment, minds concern themselves solely with the relative.

Each of us is but parts based on the lie of separation. To the degree we experience ourselves as part, we can possibly observe reality, but no part acting as part can fully perceive **Truth**. It disappears when we grasp for it through our senses, attention, and perception, for **Truth** is complete, not fragmented experiences. When we glimpse **Truth**, it dissolves any lies of separation underlying the identities or beliefs we're enacting; thus the moment we try to entirely grasp or preserve **Truth**, it escapes us.

The Absolute is both contained in each part and is the container of each part; experience can be had only in part as parts, but inevitably an expanding universe will contract and all things that are separate will rejoin and return. Whereas the cycle of any created part is circular (creation—preservation—destruction), **Truth** is the whole cycle itself cycling. Any persisting part is inside space-time, and thus any experience (or lifetime) can perceive and be perceived only in part as parts.

Truth is outside space-time and its cyclical changes, while physicality places us within the persistence and differentiation of space and time. But **Truth** is beyond persistence and differentiation, resolving all apparencies of separation. **Truth** is Absolute, existing independently and not in relation or comparison. **Truth** is.

Ask yourself . . .

■ Look within the Frame of **Truth**: What lie do you see exposed in the contents of this Frame? What **Truth** are you hiding, ignoring, repressing, or hedging?

■ The **Truth** Frame often reveals something you've judged to be true before you've looked at it entirely. What aspect of existence or yourself do you see within the Frame that you believe to be so? What might you be missing about this aspect? Is there anything that bothers or sticks or aches about it? Conversely, is there something about it that you cannot see—some part of it that seems impossible to glimpse or just out of your reach? Follow these clues to greater **Truth**.

■ Gaze into the **Truth** Frame and inquire: What partial **Truth** have you been pretending is more? What story about separateness and separation have you been finding solace in or using to make excuses? What finite aspect of yourself or your life have you been imagining is significant or essential? What aspect of your own ego has been masquerading as **Truth**?

■ Often, the **Truth** Frame directs our attention to a deception, narrative, or propaganda told to us by another or others that we believe to be **Truth**. It might be a complete fabrication, or perhaps it is a lie cloaked in authority, information, or shared belief. What do you see within the **Truth** Frame that you've accepted as **Truth** rather than looking for yourself?

■ Do you believe that **Truth** can be found only in one facet or part of existence? Are you convinced that there are viewpoints or parts of existence that must be totally devoid of **Truth**? The **Truth** Frame challenges these suppositions, inviting you to look within its contents to discover aspects of **Truth** to which you're currently blinded by your own ideas.

■ Sometimes within this Frame you'll see a **Truth** about yourself outside space and time. What do you need to confront about this **Truth**? What scares you about it? What comfort can you find in it? What change needs to happen in you or the way you live your life after glimpsing this **Truth** about yourself?

■ **Truth** nudges you to look beyond yourself, your life, and the cares of this moment. Focus on expanding past your own viewpoints, decisions, and disagreements. Exteriorize outside yourself as subject and release what surrounds you as object. Meditate upon the contents of the **Truth** Frame and then close your eyes and empty your mind, watching your emotional reactions and thoughts rise and fade away. Take the time and space you need to center, if only for the briefest moment, with **Truth**.

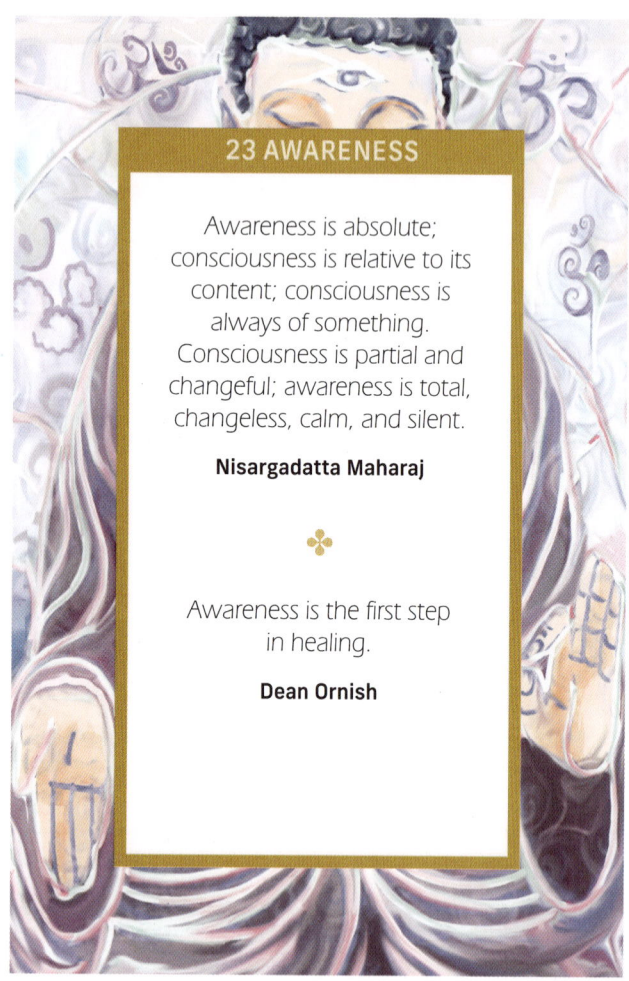

23 AWARENESS

Awareness is absolute; consciousness is relative to its content; consciousness is always of something. Consciousness is partial and changeful; awareness is total, changeless, calm, and silent.

Nisargadatta Maharaj

❖

Awareness is the first step in healing.

Dean Ornish

AWARENESS

We often use the words "consciousness" and **Awareness** interchangeably, but they are not the same thing.

Being awake and responsive to what engages our attention is consciousness. Science studies *states of consciousness*, ranging from awake to asleep. While asleep we are unconscious, as we are waking up we become conscious, and when we are awake we are conscious. However, we are conscious of far less than we perceive and aware of far more than we are conscious.

Consciousness is of the mind and physicality itself, a relative phenomenon of embodiment. When conscious, our mind prioritizes what we shall be conscious of, actively not recognizing and not knowing most of what exists in **Awareness** outside our conscious viewpoint.

In contrast, **Awareness** is before and beyond consciousness, as well as the source from which consciousness directs our focus. **Awareness** permeates everything effortlessly without viewpoint. Whereas we *become* conscious of something, we have always been aware of it. **Awareness** is outside all things, while consciousness is inside something.

We can focus consciousness, but not **Awareness**. You are always aware, even if you are not conscious that you are. In order to be conscious, you need a watcher and something being watched, but **Awareness** is devoid of subject and object. Consciousness chooses and rejects, while **Awareness** pervades and is, the state of no mind and therefore transcendence.

Ask yourself . . .

■ Gaze into the **Awareness** Frame without judgment or preference. What do you see? Try to take in everything, even the smallest details. Now soften your focus, perceiving the contents in their entirety. Sit with this experience, contemplating the impersonal All. Do you find it difficult to be aware without mental focus? Does **Awareness** make you feel restless, centered, scattered, lost, peaceful, or other emotions?

■ As you look at what you've placed within the **Awareness** Frame, do you notice some aspect of yourself reflected? Perhaps you see something you want or else believe you lack? Conversely, do you see something that is definitely *not* like you— something wrong or undesirable? Conscious minds tend to operate habitually, fixating on getting and having rather than being. Over time, **Awareness** deteriorates further as our beliefs limit our ability to see what we've decided is not or cannot be. Ask yourself: "What attitude or emotion arises within me in response to what I'm seeing?" This is your clue as to the beliefs that are limiting your **Awareness**.

■ The **Awareness** Frame requires you to broaden your vision. What are you missing in your current conscious focus? What do you see within the **Awareness** Frame that shatters your patterns or preconceptions to help you become aware of the larger vista of Presence?

■ Is there some aspect of existence contained within the **Awareness** Frame that frightens you in its otherness, detachment, or supposed danger? **Awareness** is impersonal and without investment in what is or is not. Can you see what is and what is not without judgment or attachment about what you observe, its effect on you, and how it affects what you care about? Let the **Awareness** Frame be your guide.

◼ **Awareness** reminds you that you are not your mind. How do the contents of the **Awareness** Frame demonstrate the no-mind path to Presence? Can you open to these hints to become aware of the stories you're telling yourself and that society is telling you, rather than lost in your mind's constant narration? Mindfulness is not being full of mind, but being aware of mind—dispassionately viewing the mind and all its shenanigans. Watch your thoughts in response to the **Awareness** Frame; let them arise and dissipate as you ask yourself: Who is doing the thinking? Where do thoughts come from? What is a thought? Where is your mind?

◼ Emotions are *energy-motions*, waves of feelings that remain if you resist them or give them energy. What waves of emotion wash over you as you gaze into the **Awareness** Frame? **Awareness** whispers that you are not your feelings, emotions, or attachments, for "you" exist only in context, by separation and through distinction. Pain is external stimuli; suffering is internal reaction. Can you find "I" without defining it by the identity of your mind or through comparison with what it is not? What emotions are revealed by **Awareness** that you have identified with or as yourself?

◼ **Awareness** requires quiet and stillness for most of us. Observe what's inside the **Awareness** Frame with calm, tranquility, and silence, watching and releasing what arises. Is there something there that you might not have acknowledged? Perhaps it's time to make **Awareness** a regular daily practice.

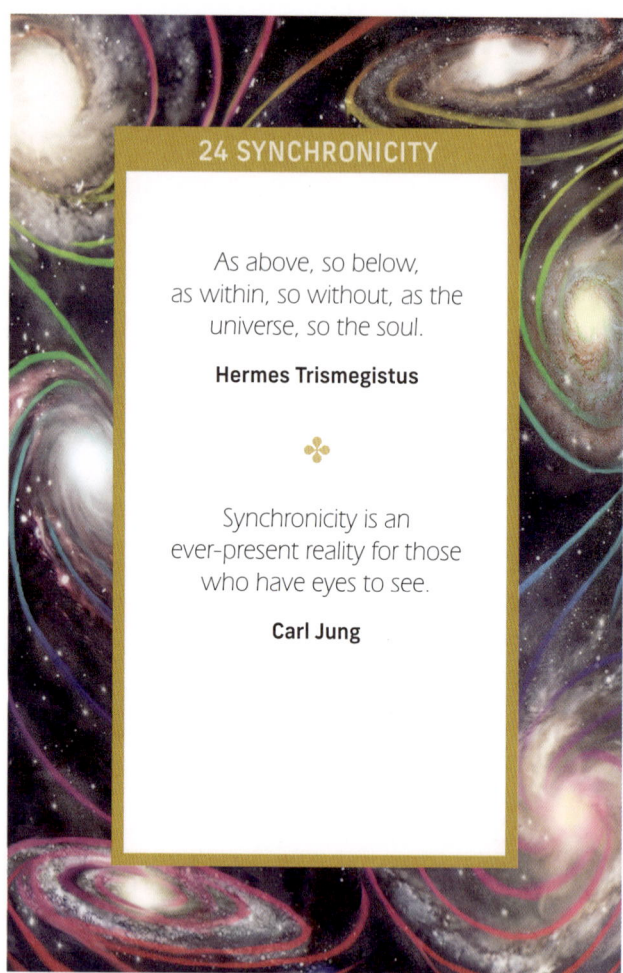

24 SYNCHRONICITY

As above, so below,
as within, so without, as the
universe, so the soul.

Hermes Trismegistus

♣

Synchronicity is an
ever-present reality for those
who have eyes to see.

Carl Jung

SYNCHRONICITY

When you gaze at the expanse of stars in the night sky, do they feel distant? Do they make you feel like you're a part of a design much grander than yourself? The closest star to Earth is Proxima Centauri, 1.5 times as large as Jupiter and 4.24 light-years away from us. This means the light we are seeing now as the bright speck named Proxima Centauri was actually produced about 4.2 years ago. For Frame of reference, the light we recognize as Polaris—the famous "North Star" that is about fifty times bigger than the sun—is 323 years old, and the star we call Betelgeuse (a whopping 950 times larger than our sun) radiated what we see during our Middle Ages. Does the sheer magnitude of size and power make you feel smaller somehow, perhaps even helpless and inconsequential? With so much time and space between us, can the stars really have any effect on our lives here and now? Is one star "better" than another? Is one star more or less vital? Do you love or hate any one of the twinkling pinpoints of light that you see more than another? If one disappeared, would you even miss it?

Conversely, consider the virus, that microscopic family of biological agents that can cause illness, even death. In comparison to the mighty spheres in the heavens, the spherical coronavirus—named for its unusual protein spikes that look like an elegant crown ("corona" in Latin)—is smaller than a particle of wildfire smoke. Yet, most of us perceive these minuscule creations as definitely having an effect on our lives. When you think of these tiny viruses that are invisible to your naked eye, do they feel distant? Do they make you feel like you're part of a design grander than yourself, or, conversely, do you feel smaller somehow, perhaps even helpless and inconsequential? Are viruses better or worse than the stars? More or less vital to existence? Do you love or hate them in comparison to stars? If coronavirus disappeared, would you miss it?

In theory, those of us who consider ourselves more spiritually focused aspire to coexistence, that beautiful ideal of existing together at the same time in peace, regardless of divergent practices or points of view. Both stars and viruses coexist at different extremes in our universe, but humans struggle to do so (especially emotionally). For us, life is personal, and to the degree that we take something or someone personally—whether we deem it good or bad—we struggle to coexist with those parts of existence that bother us, harm what we care about, or get in our way.

Synchronicity is both personal and impersonal at the same time. Both enormous and insignificant; All That Is as well as each and every thing that exists as a separate part. **Synchronicity** is creation, preservation, and destruction as an infinite symphony, the truth that we're all playing the same music together as separate instruments while at the same time Being the Conductor. We've all chosen the music and our part in the orchestra, willing the playing of our personal notes in our section as part of our orchestra with all the orchestras orchestrated throughout existence. All the little wills united in willing one great Will. But don't miss this truth—each is the sheet music, the instrument, the musician, the Conductor, and the music itself. Simultaneously. Coexistently. **Synchronistically**.

When we're living within the truth of **Synchronicity**, events and phenomena seem to align for us in perfect rhythmical order. We learn to pay attention, not from a place of personal interest but a curious sense of wonder at existence, for this present moment shall pass and never come again.

Is **Synchronicity** simply coincidence arising from confirmation bias and the human brain's basic design to identify and perceive a pattern where none exists? Or is it the one becoming many, things existing all together that really are the same thing, all acting as parts together as one Being while concurrently maintaining an awareness of conceived separateness—the feeling of being everything but not more one thing than anything else. The Frame of **Synchronicity** offers no hierarchy, no better or worse, no big or small.

Synchronicity is simply the all-in-one barbaric yawp of Being's resounding "YES!"

Ask yourself . . .

■ Is there something you need to confront about what you've placed within the **Synchronicity** Frame today, some aspect that you've deemed more or less vital, more or less worthy, more or less useful, more or less desirable, even more or less vile about existence? Use the Frame's contents to scrutinize your own systems of hierarchy, morality, and judgment. Not sure how to begin this process? Start with going into whatever evokes the strongest emotions within you, whether positive or negative. What seems closest to you, most personal to you, and why? Your personal investment exposes your prejudices and biases avoiding coexistence.

■ What patterns are repeating in your life? What are you seeing over and over that defies rational explanation? Within the **Synchronicity** Frame, discover a meaningful coincidence that surrounds you—some aspect of existence that is being repeated above, below, without, and within you that you're missing and need to acknowledge. Until you notice, acknowledge, and let go of this recurrence, these patterns will keep repeating in your life. Is there perhaps a **Synchronicity** it's time to accept and release?

■ Often, the **Synchronicity** Frame reveals an aspect of existence that you need to see more clearly within the context of All That Is. What do you see within the **Synchronicity** Frame that you might be misperceiving because you're too close to it? Does it have too much of a personal effect on your life? Conversely, is it too distant, alien, or other so that you cannot relate to it and either dismiss it outright, judge it as inferior, or make it mysterious, of greater importance, and therefore beyond you somehow?

■ Is there some aspect of existence contained within the **Synchronicity** Frame that you think should *not* exist? Do you hold yourself judge and jury over another aspect of existence, believing your own story/narrative/ordering so much that you conclude that it's superior? Are your deeply held *nots* clouding your ability to coexist, see clearly, and work with other portions of existence synergistically—what is *not* you, *not* right, *not* good, and should *not* be?

■ One insidious error about **Synchronicity** is the fabrication of meaning everywhere to serve one's own desires, needs, excuses, justifications, or beliefs. What do you glimpse within the Frame of **Synchronicity** that has captured your attention, producing an unavoidable refrain that runs through your mind and daily life? Why are you so transfixed and obsessed with it? What might happen if you still your craving for the significance and meaning you're looking for in its realization and instead choose to simply coexist with it instead?

■ Ask yourself as you gaze within the **Synchronicity** Frame if you see something you need to say "Yes!" to. Do you see an aspect of What Is that it's time to accept, affirm, support, or receive? How do you see yourself reflected in this aspect of existence? How do you see this aspect of existence manifested in you?

■ **Synchronicity** is not sympathy, yet often our initial notions of **Synchronicity** surface when we encounter another's mental state and feel an empathy or compassion for them. Everything vibrates, us included, and when we connect however subtly with the resonance of another, we experience affinity, whether star or virus. What *as above* do you see within the **Synchronicity** Frame to inform your *so below*? What *as within* do you see to inform your *so without*? What *as the universe* do you see to inform your *so the soul*?

The soul should always
stand ajar, ready to welcome
the ecstatic experience.

Emily Dickinson

The timeless in you
is aware of life's timelessness.
And knows that yesterday is
but today's memory and
tomorrow is today's dream.

Khalil Gibran

VOID

(Warning: You may find it easier to engage with this Frame after meditation, time alone in nature, a great workout, really good sex, or a bottle of wine . . .)

In theory, mystics and all sorts of religious-type persons over the years have sought or claimed to touch or reach or return to **Void**, calling it such words as nirvana, heaven, enlightenment, source, Brahman, paradise, awakening, rapture, bliss, transcendence, etc.

Void is generally defined as a completely empty space. Classically, **Void** was associated with chaos, that formless and empty primordial state said to have existed before creation in many mythologies. Of course, Ovid morphed this view of chaos in his *Metamorphoses* to mean a disordered mess, distinctly separating our modern idea of chaos from our description of **Void**.

This shared physical universe, hypothesized multiverses, other dimensions, and even one's own internal universe are located within space and time and far from empty. **Void**, however, contains nothing: no matter or form, no volume or mass or energy, no scientific or natural or human laws, *nothing*. **Void** is outside (beside? beyond?) space-time and relativity.

Void is the ultimate paradox because the minds of the created cannot understand, grasp, or have **Void**, for only when you separate a thing from itself can it become conceivable. Most of our actions, desires, goals, ends, and reactions arise from our drive to *a*-**void** the **Void.** Ennui, emptiness, nothingness, loneliness, and dissolution are common experiences upon mere brushes with **Void** and horrify most of us, and so we run away from the nothingness with all our being. Much of who and what we are (and are not) is a direct outcome of this *a-**void**-ance*. You are nearing the **Void** when you begin to lose your cares, your heartaches, your worries, your ideas . . . and most of all yourself.

Void is spirit that is not-being, static that is nonbeing—not as in a negation, but an absence both of affirmation and negation. **Void** encompasses what was, what is, and what will be, all at once. **Void** is undifferentiated potential as a part of what never was, what might have been, what is, and what will be.

The material world, on the other hand, is perceived through context, relativity, and duality. To speak of what is beautiful or right implies that their opposites—the "ugly" and "wrong"— must also exist in contrast; thus, to invoke a duality is to invoke its opposite. *Part*ial experience is but a piece-by-piece confrontation of the a**void**ance of the truth of static: **Void**.

All created things are fulfilled in **Void**; where everything that has a beginning has an end, the **Void** is what has no beginning and no end and thus was never created. **Void** is whence the dream arises and the death resolves, because experience is predicated on the separation of cycles into parts as stages. If you were to look at all cycles as one cycle as the cycles themselves cycle, so that all that has been will be, and always has been resolves—what remains is **Void**. **Void** is Infinity, the timeless Möbius outside the decision for the Möbius to exist, pure outsideness to the point of being within.

Ask yourself . . .

■ What do you see contained within the **Void** Frame? What does it mean to you? Try to take in every detail, especially those aspects you might have missed at first glance. Did you notice anything new? What do these new elements mean to you, and why do you think you didn't see them initially?

■ Now, remove the **Void** Frame, both widening and softening your attention on everything in front of you, releasing any preferences or inclinations as you can. What changes when you broaden and free your vision?

■ Attempt to let go of your focus entirely and simply exist in the experience of no Frames, no viewpoints, no attributions, no substance, no significance. Close your eyes and continue to use your entire visual field as you simply exist in this darkness, the closest thing to visual nothingness possible for a body. How does this suggestion of **Void** seem to you? How long can you remain still and silent with your eyes closed, focusing on nothing? Do you feel uncomfortable, peaceful, restless . . . or something else?

■ Finally, open your eyes and place the **Void** Frame back where it began. Do you feel relief in this restored order and focal point, or otherwise? What is vital about attention, aim, and action to the physical experience? What might be lost by our constant focusing and seeking of purpose? What is gained or lost by our Frames and reFrames?

■ One day your body will die, and your identity, your problems, and your investments will resolve into nothingness. What do you see within the **Void** Frame to suggest what you need today to continue your life's journey toward inevitable ending?

■ Do you see something you've been a**void**ing revealed within the **Void** Frame? It's time to face, acknowledge, confront, and relinquish this burden of a**void**ance.

■ Are you adrift in ennui, a feeling of listlessness and dissatisfaction arising from a lack of occupation or excitement? **Void** Frames the cause of this unrest reflected in yourself and what you see. How much of your life is lived to escape **Void** or create drama and meaning in your life in order to feel more? How much of what you say, do, and have is to a**void** emptiness, loneliness, or meaninglessness?

Void is the ultimate paradox because the minds of the created cannot understand, grasp, or have Void, for only when you separate a thing from itself can it become conceivable.

THE WORLD.

WORKING WITH THE OPEN WINDOW

Most backs of oracle and Tarot decks seem to be mere afterthoughts to the deck's creation and message. Often simplistic and forgettable, occasionally reversible, and sometimes composed of pretty artwork, card backs are rarely as meaningful as the rest of the deck's images. I've experimented with lots of oracles, but I've never before seen the image on the back of the deck have an *equally* important message as a tool for its user.

The **Open Window** on the back of each card in *Frame This Oracle* is a Frame with a vital and profound communication in and of itself. **Open Window** represents you as a divine window, your personal Frame, your own unique individual viewpoint in this particular space and time of embodiment.

Work with the **Open Window** when you're struggling to differentiate yourself, your inner world, and your perspective from those around you and your environment. Use it deliberately with this intention or, contrariwise, consider using the backside of the deck as the Frame you're intended to work with today if the **Open Window** seems to "pop" out at you while shuffling or choosing a card at random.

Ask yourself . . .

■ Contemplate the contents of the **Open Window** to see the focal points of your own personal Frame reflected. What Frames that you're creating for yourself are revealed within your **Open Window**? How might your Frame be shaping you, your reactions to your environment, your feelings about your life as well as how you choose to live it, and what you focus on among all that can be experienced?

You are the window through which you must see the world.

George Bernard Shaw

❖

Two men look out a window. One sees mud, the other sees the stars.

Oscar Wilde

■ When you look at what you've placed within the **Open Window**, what does it suggest about external events and people that have shaped your own personal Frame? What stories do you see disclosed that you're telling yourself about life and living? What personal traumas and triumphs are exposed that have focused your attention on certain things and away from other choices or encounters? How is your Frame different or similar to those around you? Who agrees with your Frame and who doesn't? How is your current framing steering you toward some aspects of existence and away from others right now?

■ Do you see within the **Open Window** Frame anything that is inhibiting your own framing in any way? Does the **Open Window** show an idea that constrains whom and what you care about, limits what you focus on, hinders where you will go, or restricts how you will live?

■ The contents of the **Open Window** Frame often display the image or parts of yourself that you're deliberately framing and presenting to the world as "you." How accurate is this artfully rendered version of yourself and the world as you wish it to be? Does your present Frame suit you, or is it time to change it, time to redecorate?

■ Do you see anything revealed within the **Open Window** Frame that you absolutely do *not* wish others to see about you and your world? How does this seem to you? Is there anything your Frame is actively hiding—any cracks in your wall that the Frame misdirects others' attention from perceiving?

■ Is there anything you see in the **Open Window** that your personal Frame is protecting? Is there anything you're framing that you don't wish to Frame? Is there anything you've focused your attention on that you don't wish to do?

■ When you look at what you've placed within the **Open Window**, do you like what it reveals about the aspects of existence that you're focused on at present? Is it time for a reFrame, or does the **Open Window** reaffirm your focus and present trajectory?

*The window has a wonderful view of a lake,
but the view doesn't view itself.*

Wisława Szymborska

You hold within your hands a tool—deliberately and carefully crafted—to help you see yourself, your life, those around you, and existence itself more clearly each and every time you use it.

The power to command attention transfixes us today. *Frame This Oracle* will refocus the almighty power of your attention away from what generally engrosses you, whether mindlessly or obsessively—away from virtual media, what other people think, what you've been taught to believe, what you've decided must be so (or mustn't be), what seems to matter—and allow you to perceive what you've been missing.

Be prepared to realize you've been missing a profound amount in the process.

Perhaps—gasp!—even allow yourself to be bored as you use this tool. How often do we allow ourselves to be bored in this modern world of distractions? Immerse yourself in the luxury of boredom, of not-doing, and maybe even nondoing, for it is the gift of boredom that forces you to be alone with yourself—your own focus, your own frame of attention and reference, along with the many thoughts that you think are your own. On the other side of boredom sits emptiness, refocusing our individual lens so we can begin to see through fresh Frames.

Any good oracle or Tarot deck contains many different truths about existence—most if not all obvious to us at some level. But no one can put their attention upon the whole of existence all at once. The more All we are, the less one we can be. One diffuses . . . disappears in the face of All . . . and the things that cause an individual to thrive dissolve in the face of Everything All at Once. We can have moments of vast bodhisattva seeing and mountaintop experiences wherein we

139

see far beyond our simplistic identities, but there is no focus in that. This is precisely why yogis need to be hand-fed and cleaned by someone else in samadhi, why people on extreme psychedelic drug trips often die or do things that eventually cause their own deaths: the vastness of All is in opposition to the singular survival of one.

Work with *Frame This Oracle* to rediscover the fullness of experience, to exercise the capacity to be totally attentive, to be subjectively immersed in one viewpoint at a time and in a particular space instead of objectively All Points All Together. One point/part/focus is the fullest experience of being (rather than Being).

This vital tool can also help you glimpse the social imaginary we are all creating together—what we collectively believe to be and what we communally wish to be, as opposed to what actually is. Practice using these Frames as a means to reflect on life and the world we live in, instead of merely thinking and acting unconsciously in accordance with the way we've imagined the world to be, bombarded by more and more socially acceptable Frames fabricated by a society preoccupied with placing each one *just so*, to cover the ever-broadening cracks in our plaster.

Frame This Oracle is a philosophical and metaphysical tool of discovery rather than a predictive one, although the more you see accurately, the greater your ability to predict.

Finally, this is a tool for communication, to hear your own and other voices or messages, to transform your ability to sense and receive. Use it to hone your own untapped skills of perception.

Pulling one Frame and looking through the truth of its perspective gives us the chance we need to focus, so that our *one* self can use the power of attention to alchemically transform itself in the direction that new truth points us. And rather than impotently dispersing in all directions, we can aim in one specific direction carefully through our pointed power of focus to, we hope, hit our mark.

Your precious Frame is a sacred gift with boundless potential for epiphanies, revelations, and visions. Find the story you wish to live before you, and go forth to live a focused life, keeping your sights on what you deem worthy to put a Frame around.

—Juno Lucina, December 11, 2022

People are like stained-glass windows.

Elisabeth Kübler-Ross

The highest form of human excellence is to question oneself and others.

Socrates

AFTERWORD

by the **ARCHANGEL ZADKIEL**

Dear one,

There will never be another spirit quite like yours in all of existence; with this truth comes great possibility and even greater responsibility.

Life is directional, not an endpoint. It is your aim that matters, not the dips or crests along the way. What you feel most deeply, most acutely, are the dips and the crests, but it is the way itself that determines your course and, therefore, your destiny.

Passion arises from intention. Compassion arises from extension. Dispassion arises from expansion.

You are vital to existence, as is every soul you encounter.

You bless and so you are blessed.

You reject and so you are rejected.

You harm and so you are harmed.

You love and so you are loved.

What you seek you become. What you avoid voids you.

What you frame separates you, defines you, names you, provokes you.

Frame wisely, for what you choose to place within your frames forgives your past, inspires your present, and promises your future.

Juno Lucina is the pen name of the award-winning author of *The Healing Tarot* (illustrated by Monica Knighton) as well as *The Kingdom Within Tarot* and *The Alchemy of Tarot* (both with illustrator Shannon ThornFeather). You can explore Juno's articles in periodicals like The Cartomancer and The Esotoracle magazines; she's also a popular thought-provoking featured speaker at cartomancy events. Watch for her eerie yet enlightening metaphysical novels under the pseudonym Rose Guildenstern. Ever fluid and changing, Juno is more a verb than a noun, more an introduction than a conclusion; Juno is just a Story pointing the Way. Connect at www.roseandjuno.com

Dan Goodfellow is a visionary artist, druid, and proud member of the Avalonian tradition based in his native Glastonbury, UK. Dangoodfellow.co.uk